Instructor's Guide for
the Middle School Course

Building a Bridge to Your Future

Developing the
Skills and Intrinsic Motivation Necessary to Succeed in
High School, College, & the Workforce

By Mindy Bingham and Karen Miles, M.S.
Edited by Tanja Easson

Academic Innovations
St. George, Utah

An optional curriculum component of the ***Get Focused...Stay Focused!™ Initiative***

Copies of this instructor's guide, along with the Student Workbook are available from the publisher. Visit www.academicinnovations.com or call (800) 967-8016 for information.

ISBN 978-1-878787-58-3

Published by Academic Innovations, LLC
(800) 967-8016 FAX (800) 967-4027
www.academicinnovations.com
info@academicinnovations.com
My10yearPlan.com® is a registered trademark of Academic Innovations

10 9 8 7 6 5 4 3 2 1

Manufactured in the United States of America

Contents

Building a Bridge to Your Future Instructor's Guide

Introduction

The middle school bridge workbook, ***Building a Bridge to Your Future***, was designed to do three very important things:

1. To prepare students to engage in the career exploration, career decision-making, and career planning process in high school.
2. To raise the self-efficacy of students in order for them to believe that they can be successful in high school and beyond.
3. To introduce them to the 10-year planning process and get them enthused about this process as they enter high school.

The curriculum was designed as a bridge to the ***Career Choices*** curriculum being offered as part of the Freshman Transition course in 9th grade in high schools across America. However, some students entering high school may find the requirement to develop a 10-year Plan for high school, college/post-secondary, and the workforce daunting without some kind of preparation. This bridge program provides an opportunity for them to think about the importance of having a long-range plan, and to understand that without a career and education plan, they are not in control of their future lives.

Additionally, too many middle school students believe that they will not be successful in high school. But this is a fallacy. This curriculum covers numerous topic areas designed for students to understand more about their attitudes, self-concept, self-motivation, and self-management. Understanding how they think about learning and life gives them important strategies and helps them see how, in using them, they can be successful in their future academic life and work life. This content falls squarely in Bloom's Affective Domain: "growth in feelings or emotional areas (attitude or self)."

The student workbook contain a pre- and post-test to ascertain the effectiveness of this curriculum as an intervention. These are designed to assess whether there is an increased level of readiness to engage in the career development process; and to assess whether there is perceived increased self-efficacy. The quiz "How ready are you to think about your future?" on page 168–169 is very brief, but please allow adequate time for the students to reflect on their feelings in the "What have I learned?" response at the end of the workbook on page 168–169. This will give students time to reflect on what they have learned, and will give you, the teacher, an opportunity to validate their improved level of readiness to engage in career exploration and decision-making, and their increased self-efficacy as successful students.

In addition, the Checkpoint: **What are My Next Steps?** on page 165 in Chapter 12 of the Workbook could be used as your final exam. This is a preliminary plan for each student as they enter high school. You want them to give this project the attention required to make it meaningful.

It is hoped that you, the teacher, enjoy teaching this curriculum, as you help your students to have a better understanding of themselves and their future possible selves. By guiding your students in an exploration of this content, you are helping them to take their first steps towards their dreams of the future. They will thank you for it because of the transformation this will make in each life. You are making a difference!

Section 1

Quick Start Guide
Instructor Success Checklist

To better prepare your students for success in high school, career planning readiness and higher self-efficacy, it is important to remember that your ***Building a Bridge to Your Future*** coursework should be:

- Comprehensive, with class discussion and active learning as the key delivery methods
- Rigorous review the appropriate pages in Section 4 of this instructor's guide on a daily basis for instructional strategies
- Sequential, completed in order from beginning to end—Chapters 1 to 12
- Delivered with at least 45 hours of class time focused on the ***Building a Bridge to Your Future*** lessons
- Taught by an instructor who is well-prepared and enthusiastic about the course

In preparing for this course:

Your Lead Teacher and team of ***Building a Bridge to Your Future*** instructors meet to begin planning for implementation at your school.

- ☐ Watch a video of author Karen Miles talk about the course and its goals. This can be found on the Teachers' Lounge.
- ☐ Read this instructor's guide for a complete overview of the course delivery options.
- ☐ In particular review Section 4 of this guide, which includes lesson presentation ideas for each of the activities in the student workbook.
- ☐ Develop a pacing guide for the complete course, prior to beginning your first day of class, so you know how much time you have to spend on the lessons. See pages 3/4 to 3/13 and Section 6 of this guide.

Between now and the first day of class, finalize your lesson plans.

Based on:

1. The time you have to complete your course,
2. Your program goals, and/or
3. Your academic discipline.

- Develop your pacing guide for your course. An example can be found 3/4.
- **Read through the *Building a Bridge to Your Future* student workbook and thoroughly review Section 4 of this instructor's guide** making note of the content selected. At this point you may choose to edit and enhance the lessons based on your school's particular goals and your student population.
- **Meet with your school's team of *Building a Bridge to Your Future* teachers and your Lead Teacher.**
  - Going lesson by lesson (Section 4), brainstorm and finalize your strategies for delivery. Your ***Building a Bridge to Your Future*** instructional team can be a great support system for daily and weekly evaluation. Share what works for you, strategies you may try, and challenges you encounter.
- **Review the pre- and post-survey** (pages 11 and 12 in the ***Building a Bridge to Your Future* workbook)** so you are ready to administer these at the appropriate times. The pre-surveys are done prior to any work in the workbook. The post-surveys are done after students have completed the workbook.

IMPORTANT: Homework assignments are critical to course success.

- As a comprehensive guidance course, it is important to set high expectations from the first day of class. This is a rigorous class. The more students put into it, the more they'll get out of it.
- Homework assignments help to prepare students for the day's discussion and provide the space for reflection of their own thoughts, goals, plans, and attitudes about the lesson for the day. Class time is then used for discussions, energizers, brainstorming, and group activities as noted in this instructor's guide.
- Be sure to thoroughly review homework at the time it is assigned.

Once your class starts:

First few days of class

- Administer the pre-survey s when you hand out the books. The pre-surveys are available on pages 11 and 12 of the workbook.

Daily

- Review your pacing guide **spreadsheet.** Section 6
- Turn to the corresponding page(s) in Section 4 of this instructor's guide and review the recommendations for that activity or exercise. The course is content-rich and rigorous, while providing relevance and helping students build relationships (with themselves, others, and the world). You'll need to finely tune your delivery and timing for each lesson. See yourself as a discussion leader, mentor, coach, and cheerleader, helping students develop and explore their own vision of a productive future.
- **Assign homework from their Building a *Bridge to Your Future Workbook*,** so students come to class prepared for discussion and group activities.

Weekly

- **Meet with your team of *Building a Bridge to Your Future* instructors and Lead Administrator/Teacher** to discuss presentation of activities and to brainstorm solutions to challenges. Occasionally invite your principal and district leaders to attend.

Throughout the course

- **For personalized support and professional development resources,** remember that we are here to help. Contact our Curriculum Support team at (800) 967-8016 or support@academicinnovations.com.

Final project

Checkpoint: **What are My Next Steps,** starting on page 165 of the workbook, can be used as a final project. It can be developed into a preliminary plan for students as they enter high school. If they are meeting with counselors prior to their freshman year, encourage them to share this project with their counselors. This will provide data to their guidance counselors, so their advice can be personalized for each student.

Final assessment

- **Assign the post-surveys after students complete the workbook.** When comparing the results from the pre- and post-survey, it is expected that students will have had a shift in attitude and self-efficacy about their ability to tackle career decision-making in high school. The reflective essay may be more revealing than the self-assessment. When reviewing the students' comments in the essays, look for themes mentioned by many in the class, adjectives that are repeated by multiple students to describe their feelings/attitude, etc.

At the end of the course or school year

- **Share your experience** with Academic Innovations by completing an online teacher survey found on the Teachers' Lounge. We take these evaluations seriously and it helps us upgrade the services we offer you.

How to Use This Guide

Your first thought after being handed this guide might be, oh my goodness, why is this so large? Do I need to know all this to teach this course? The answer is no.

This instructor's guide was designed to provide comprehensive support to the instructors of the ***Building a Bridge to Your Future*** curriculum, school and district administrators and program managers, interested in implementing curriculum that will impact high school performance and beyond.

Naturally, you'll want to start by reviewing the table of contents. Focus on the sections providing information and resources applicable to your job or current tasks.

*For **Building a Bridge to Your Future** Instructors*

We recommend that you carefully review the following sections throughout your preparation and implementation process:

Section 1: Quick Start
Section 2: Developing Self-directed Lifelong Learners
Section 3: Course Options: Determining Your Course Structure
Section 4: Lesson Plan Suggestions for Each Activity
Section 5: Getting Buy-in: The First Vital Step
Section 6: DevelopingYour Pacing Guide
Section 7: Instructional Strategies
Section 8: Assessment

For Administrators or Program Managers

If you are responsible for overseeing implementation of the curriculum, we recommend a thorough review of the following sections:

Section 1: Quick Start
Section 2: Developing Self-directed Lifelong Learners
Section 3: Course Options: Determining Your Course Structure
Section 5: Getting Buy-in: The First Vital Step

Curriculum and Technical Support

Academic Innovations believes that our responsibility only begins with your adoption of our course materials. To help ensure your success and the success of your students, we have created a variety of professional development options, curriculum support programs, and online resources.

You also have access to the most valuable of resources: Our dedicated staff, volunteer educators, and consultants who stand ready to support you via phone, email, or online meeting. A quick call to our office between 9:00 AM and 4:00 PM (Mountain Time) will put you in touch with someone who can answer your unique question.

Curriculum and Technical Support
(800) 967-8016

Section 2

Developing Self-directed Lifelong Learners

Envisioning a productive future = College* completion AND Workplace success

College and Career Readiness

> *The national conversation around education has shifted from baseline academic proficiency to preparation for the rigors of college and the workplace. This shift comes as many college faculty and employers note that students graduating from American high schools are not prepared for post-secondary education or workplace demands.*
>
> — The Alliance for Excellent Education, Washington, DC

Lack of college readiness is demonstrated by low college attendance rates, low college graduation rates, and high post-secondary remediation costs.

Yet by 2018, 62% of jobs are expected to require some level of post-secondary training, according to a 2009 study by the Georgetown University Center on Education and the Workforce. More students than ever are enrolling in college, but research reveals that an astonishing percentage of students drop out. According to a 2011 report released by the Pathways to Prosperity Project at the Harvard Graduate School of Education, only 56% of college students pursuing four-year degrees finish within six years, and only 29% of those who start two-year degrees complete them within three years.

Our country has long promoted the economic benefits of a college degree and touted college as a necessity for all students. Unfortunately, until recently not nearly enough attention has been focused on whether or not students actually finished college. As it turns out, we have failed to sufficiently prepare students for college, overlooking the skills, resources, and support necessary to ensure successful completion. Students have come to perceive getting into college as the ultimate goal but have no plan for how to succeed there, often not truly understanding why they are even in college. And, with an overemphasis on the four-year degree as the ideal option, we set many students up for failure when a two-year or technical program would serve them better.

As a result, college completion rates are abysmal.

Career and Education Plans: Critical to College Completion

Yet, according to "Advancing Student Success in the California Community Colleges" by the California Community Colleges Student Success Task Force:

> *Research from the Institute for Higher Education Leadership and Policy shows that students who entered a program [of study] in their first year were twice as likely to complete a certificate, degree or transfer as students who entered a program after their first year.*

*Throughout this manual the term, ***College*** includes all post-secondary options for advanced education and training. Certification in many vocations can be just as valuable and satisfying as a four-year degree.

The Student Success Task Force also found that guidance is essential for students to achieve their potential:

> *The current matriculation model assumes that students will clarify their educational objective in the course of meeting with a counselor. However, many students never see a counselor… Helping students make informed choices about their education is a critical strategy to help increase student success...*

The task force goes on to recommend that:

> *Students who arrive without a clear goal need an education plan that allows them to systematically define their educational needs and objectives and explore their options… Expanded resources for career exploration are essential.*

Why Wait—Start in Middle School

In order for students to successfully carry out career exploration and career decision-making in high school, they have to be ready to engage in those activities. This middle school curriculum helps students to understand the need to think about career planning in high school, as many of the decisions they make about their futures will take place during that time, either as a result of what they choose to do (taking Career Technical Education classes, AP classes, etc.), or do not participate in. Either way they are affecting their futures. Their attitudes about learning and planning for their futures, and their beliefs about themselves, will make a difference to their success in high school and beyond.

Intrinsic Motivation: Vital to Academic Success

Getting the unfocused, under-motivated student to embrace the rewards of education has long been a primary goal of education reform and redesign. The efforts of qualified, experienced instructors with quality instructional materials in well-funded programs are still stymied if students are unmotivated.

After all, **learning requires intrinsic motivation**, which is only possible when the learner internalizes the rewards inherent to a task and has a realistic expectation of success. Intrinsically motivated students are more likely to understand that academic achievement is not determined by luck or natural talent. They understand that they alone can control their educational attainment by expending an appropriate amount of time and energy.

The ***Building a Bridge to Your Future*** curriculum aims to change negative student attitudes around the importance of learning and their ability to succeed in high school. They will be able to identify their intrinsic motivators after taking this class.

Common Core State Standards: An Opportunity for Change

With the advent of the Common Core State Standards, instructors across the country are meeting this challenge by "repackaging" traditional disciplines. By infusing real-world themes and issues, the core content when presented as conceptualize by the developers delivers with a fresher, more relevant slant. The Common Core State Standards require instructors to change not only the way they teach, but also what they teach. Old lesson plans must be retired in favor of new course material that, as reported in January 2012 by *Education Week*:

> *...focuses on the application of knowledge in authentic situations... Teachers will need to employ instructional strategies that integrate critical and creative thinking, collaboration, problem-solving, research and inquiry, and presentation and demonstration skills.*

Flipping the college decision-making paradigm

You may have programs or coursework on your campus where you are already talking about college and which campus to attend. That is the wrong conversation to have right now for your middle school students. Why you say?

Ask any adult, regardless of their education level, to recount how they approached the three choices—major, college, career. Ask them to describe, in order, which they choose first, then second and finally last.

They will probably tell you that the first thing they chose was the college they wanted to attend. They might have picked a parent's alma mater, a party school, the one as far away from their parents as possible, or the one by the ocean or in a big city. After choosing a college, most settle next on a major, but usually not until they have attended for a couple of semesters. That choice is too often driven by what they were interested in at that time, the requirement by the college that it was "time" to choose in order to begin division classes or maybe even coaxed by a best friend to "major together."

Finally, somewhere near or even after graduation, if they made it that far, they picked their career, and embarked onto the job to market, expecting to get hired. In today's economy that is a rude awakening for student and parent alike. Today 8.5 percent of college graduates are unemployed or 16.8 percent are underemployed one year after graduation, according to The Economic Policy Institute in Washington, D.C.

Your final question, particularly if your interviewee has been out of school for many decades: "Do you think graduating high school students today make the same choices in the same order?" The answer is a resounding yes.

Then ask them, as self-aware, mature adults today, what the selection order should have been. The answer is shocking in its simplicity and it only takes moments for the person questioned to come up with the answer. Career first, major second, and college third. The order makes sense. Your career dictates what major to pursue, which in turn defines which colleges are appropriate. It is an ah-ha moment for most. Now they get it, but for many it's too late.

The problem isn't that students are not going to college; the problem is that they are not finishing. They are not finishing often because they find out they don't like their major or don't see the point of further education, they lose interest, and then decide to "figure it out later." President Obama set a goal of the U.S. having the highest percentage of college graduates in the world by 2020. How do we get there? Start career planning earlier.

Career planning cannot start in the junior year of college. The research is clear: Students who enter college with an informed declared major are far more likely to graduate (by double), than those who wander through the maze of educational choices. At a time when education leaders are engaged in discussions about college completion, free community college and performance-based funding, some of the most obvious and effective solutions are right in front of us.

This simple flip of the college decision-making paradigm is how every student in America should approach their education. In high school, the opportunity for student to participate in the *Get Focused...Stay Focused!* ™ program will provide ninth grade students with a semester (90-hour) or yearlong (180-hour) comprehensive guidance course to help them identify their interests and life goals, discover a career aligned to those interests and goals, and begin a unique skills-based 10-year education plan to prepare for that career. In some schools, students can receive college credit for the class. And in some districts in California, the 10-year Plan is required for graduation.

During the 10th, 11th, and 12th grades students take a series of follow-up 16-lesson instructional modules that help them expand their career and education options and learn the process for selecting and applying to college or post-secondary training, identifying the skills needed for their chosen career and the plan required to get those skills both in the classroom and in the community.

This program goes beyond high school. There is a new mobile app, which facilitates the continuance of the career and education planning process. Students now have a tool to easily share their plans with advisors, counselors, friends and family. When inspiration strikes and a GFSF graduate learns something new, he or she can continue the self-discovery process of updating their 10-year Plan on their mobile device.

Schools who adopt this program make a commitment of from 90 to 140 hours of classroom time over four years, starting with the freshman course and later in the follow-up modules. It is not difficult to integrate the lessons, because they are academically based and meet the Common Core state standards.

The results make the commitment well worth it. Upon completion of the program, *Get Focused...Stay Focused!* students identify and graduate with:

- A carefully considered career path
- An informed major or program of study
- A post-secondary institution or training program that not only matches their career and life goals but is affordable
- A unique Skills-based Education Plan that facilitates successful entry into a highly competitive workforce upon completion of their education.

A Video to Share

For a five-minute video intended for educators and parents, visit www.getfocusedstayfocused.org/flip.

Consider showing this *Flipping the College Decision-making Paradigm* video at your next staff meeting and parents meeting.

Get Focused...Stay Focused! An Overview

> This *Building a Bridge for Your Future* program was designed as a bridge/transitional program to your high school's *Get Focused...Stay Focused!* ™ program. Because of that you'll want to understand what your students' next steps in high school will be.

The *Get Focused...Stay Focused!* ™ Initiative is designed to provide every student with the necessary information and experiences to develop college and career readiness skills as well as facilitate the development of an online 10-year Career & Education Plan.

Begun in 2009 as an expansion of the collaboration between the dual enrollment program at Santa Barbara City College—co-winner of the 2013 Aspen Prize for Community College Excellence—and local secondary schools, the purpose of the Initiative is to ensure that:

- All incoming 9th grade students take a standards-based, *comprehensive guidance* course that culminates with an online 10-year career and education plan,
- Followed by the *systematic updating and expanding* of the 10-year plan in the 10th, 11th, and 12th grade academic classrooms, meeting the English Language Arts Common Core Standards.

In order to promote student engagement and motivation, and therefore college completion:

- Students enter their other post-secondary education institution with an *informed* declared major, a *meaningful* education plan, and a *career- focused* program of study.
- The online 10-year plan will be a common advisory and academic coaching tool used by counselors and instructors alike on both the high school and the college campus.

Sample goals for such a program include:

- Increase engagement, academic achievement, and attendance of *all* students
- Reduce suspension, expulsion, and dropout rates
- Increase the percentage of students that graduate from high school, continue their education at a college or university, and enter their post-secondary education institution with college and career ready skills.

Many of the GFSF high schools have developed their courses as dual credit opportunities through collaboration with their local community college or university.

An Overview of the Freshman Course and Follow-up Modules

Your middle school students will take this series of courses once they enter high school.

What makes the ***Career Choices*** curriculum unique and effective? Quite simply, its effectiveness is the result of its careful design: **Academically-based and repackaged in a thematic format, it addresses the developmental needs of the early adolescent while delivering on the goals of increased academic standards.** How?

- It teaches a critical decision-making process for evaluating life-defining choices.
- It culminates in the development of a 10-year career and education plan that helps young people envision a productive life of their own choosing.
- At the same time, it coaches students as they answer a pressing and crucial question: Why do I need a good education?
- It is different by design and, therefore, less threatening for all students?
- It melds high tech with high touch, an important component when seeking student buy-in of the content and concepts presented.

The bottom line: By changing attitudes, it changes lives!

Whether your students are headed for an Ivy League college or an entry-level job, they crave a clear sense of direction for their lives. A required class based on the Standards for a Freshman Transition Course from The George Washington University can help students develop a personalized, career-inclusive 10-year education plan. As they work through the coursework, students learn a self-discovery and planning process that culminates with a plan to:

- Make high school graduation a reality
- Enter and **complete** college or post-secondary education and training
- Transition into a productive and self-sufficient adulthood

This interactive freshman course captures the attention of ALL students, because at its core are the issues of the greatest importance to teens: **themselves and their future.**

In addition, this semester or year-long course can include the integration of academics and technology, making personal mastery of these skills relevant to students' lives.

Known as the decade of transition, between age 14 and 24 is probably one of the most critical decision- making periods in anyone's life. High school freshmen start making choices that will impact the rest of their lives, often without realizing it. Some of these choices have far-reaching consequences: to stay in school or not; to go to college after high school or not; to become sexually active or not; to apply focused energy to school work or not.

When young people have a **productive vision of their future** that correlates with their goals, identity, aptitudes, lifestyle expectations, and passions AND a **10-year plan of their own making built around quantitative education and career goals**, the value of working hard in school and acquiring adequate education or training becomes abundantly clear. Essentially, the **process** taught in this standards-based course quantifies the **reason to learn.**

Changing Attitudes, Changing Lives!

In four words, that sums up the goal of the ***Career Choices*** curriculum. What began as a passion for author Mindy Bingham has grown into a mission for the 40 plus individuals who write, administer, support, and train in this curriculum.

To date, over 5,000 schools and programs with nearly two million students have used ***Career Choices***.

When ***Career Choices*** was first published in 1990, it was considered a cutting edge curriculum because it integrated the theme of career, life, and educational planning into the traditional subjects of English/language arts, math, and social studies. Using an interdisciplinary approach grounded in real-life activities, students found the answer to the age-old question: "Why is education important?"

Can the Career Choices *coursework be adopted in the 8th grade and this middle school coursework implemented in the 7th grade?*

Yes, the ***Career Choices*** textbook, workbook and **My10yearPlan.com** can be adopted for the 8th grade. A number of middle schools have implemented this course over the years and that is a valid strategy. If you choose this route we recommend it as a year-long course so your studetns have more time to process the information. Sample 180-hour lesson plans are available on the ***Career Choices*** **Teachers' Lounge**.

If your high school is not going to adopt the *Get Focused...Stay Focused!* ™ program, and you chose this alternative route, we suggest that before you implement that strategy you first have a discussion with your high school leadership. Will they support your students online 10-year plans in their counseling and advisory sessions? Will they consider infusing the lessons of the follow-up modules in their academic courses (16 hours per year)? Ideally you'd like that to happen so your student's 10-year planning continues all the way through high school.

Our curriculum support team can facilitate an online meeting/webinar with your middle school/high school leadership to discuss the opportunities and answer any questions about these options. Contact us at (800) 967-8016.

Overview of the *Career Choices* Textbook, Workbook, and My10yearPlan.com® Activities

Throughout this middle school coursework, your students will learn about the online 10-year plan they will be developing in high school. What follows is an in-depth overview of that material. This information is provided so in the event you are asked any questions by your students or their parents about the 10-year planning processes you have a general understanding of what they will experience.

An important goal of the freshman course is to help students develop a 10-year education and career plan. It's critical that they evaluate their choices based on what would make *them* feel successful. As we all know, success is a very individualized measurement. Personal success is simply the fulfillment of what makes you happiest.

In this process of developing a comprehensive 10-year plan, students will learn important strategies and formulas for a decision-making process that can be used when making any life-defining decisions. Because it's a systematic process, it's important to remember that the text follows a strict order. Information and data discovered in earlier chapters are used in later ones as students continue on the path to develop their *quantitative* and *meaningful* 10-year plans.

Quantitative, naturally, is something that is definable, usually associated with a measurement. In Chapter 12, where students compile all their data, information, and insights, what they put together in the form of action plans are indeed measurable. After all, how else can success be determined?

Meaningful is an operative word. Students invest over 100 hours of study, discussion, contemplation, and work on this self-discovery journey. Each student's resulting 10-year plan will be individualized, born out of their discoveries and "ah ha" moments. The carefully planned scope and sequence of the curriculum builds on earlier discoveries in a step- by-step process. Students systematically tackle issues and topics that most people learn about the hard way. As students develop a deeper self-knowledge, you'll introduce them to increasingly sophisticated concepts with which many adults still struggle.

Because the plan is personalized, of each student's own creation, they take ownership and are connected to its outcome. This is very important. Unlike a computer-based planning process that can appear to be "magical," using plans born out of their own efforts and analysis helps students understand at a gut level the rewards of following through. By completing ***Career Choices***, they're also exposed to the consequences of *not* following through with their plans. This is important because, when the first roadblock inevitably presents itself, they're more likely to buckle down and do whatever is necessary to accomplish their goals instead of quitting or falling back to a safe position. Their motivation will be intrinsic, which is the best kind of motivation.

One of the goals of the middle school program is to introduce the 10-year planning process and get students excited about the possibilities and rewards. Speak of the 10-year plan with reverence in your class. By developing people who are long-range thinkers, you'll change your students' lives.

An important first step for your course is letting your students know from the very beginning that the culmination of the course—the product of their work—is the development of their own 10-year plan. This will become one of the most important documents they have.

We suggest that you enthusiastically introduce the 10-year plan by providing them with a vision of what it is and why it is important to their lives.

The textbook is different than others you've seen. Using a dialectic style (i.e., discussion) rather than didactic (i.e., lecturing) is the secret to success with ***Career Choices***. Instead of reading great amounts of didactic text, students learn by reflection, analysis, and research as they come up with their own personalized answers to the questions in the activities and exercises.

If you don't have a copy of the ***Career Choices*** series textbook (***Career Choices*** or ***Career Choices and Changes***) you might want to ask your school librarian to get one. Then using the content that follows, review this overview to understand what your students will experience in their freshman year.

Chapter 1—*Envisioning Your Future: How Do You Define Success?*

Chapter 1 of ***Career Choices*** opens with four fanciful stories about personalities known to students. These fantasies are about the moment these individuals discovered their life's work. As the text on page 12 goes on to explain, planning your life based on luck or magic is probably not a good option. It is here your students are exposed, for the first time, to the formula for success:

Vision + Energy = Success

This formula sums up what this course is all about: envisioning a productive and satisfying future and then creating the plans for achieving that vision so they know where to focus their energy.

Students articulate the visions of each of the celebrities (based on the story and what they know about them). Students then imagine what the celebrities did, the energy they expended both in school and at work, to accomplish their goals. This is the first of many times they will practice this life skill.

They try to envision their own futures. For many, this is difficult. However, an important part of learning is first determining what you don't know. You'll learn a lot through your students' responses to this activity. The harder it is for them to detail a realistic future, the more at-risk that student is of dropping out of high school, college, or life. While you don't want to say that to them, keep that in mind as you individualize your work with each student.

Throughout the course, you'll be asking your students over and over again to expand their vision of the future in a variety of areas. The activities and exercises they're exposed to constantly prompt them to think into the future. Through case studies of others and personalized exercises, they're asked to stretch their focus to imagine their future lives.

The topics presented include:

- Why people work, where students discover it's about more than just money
- A rubric for defining success that helps students realize it's a personal definition and make their first attempt at defining success for themselves
- The different ways people make career choices; it becomes clear that having a rational process for making what could possibly be the second most important decision in their lives is the best way to go

Making choices that are right for each person is what the ***Career Choices*** curriculum is all about. Before you can choose what you want, you need to know who you are, which leads us to Chapter 2.

Chapter 2—*Your Personal Profile: Getting What You Want Starts with Knowing Who You Are*

Ralph Waldo Emerson once observed, "Self-trust is the first secret of success." Without a basic understanding of their own personality traits, values, skills, and passions, individuals can't hope to consistently make life decisions that are personally fulfilling.

There is a Personal Profile chart that students will attempt to complete. It will be difficult for most, but they'll soon discover that the activities that follow provide experiences to help them identify their traits, characteristics, and aptitudes.

As your students work through the various trigger activities, they'll learn to determine and articulate their passions, work values, personality and strengths, skills and aptitudes, and their roles. They'll gather important data about themselves that they'll use not only throughout the balance of the course but also throughout their lives.

Students discover and communicate the many layers that make up their unique identities. As they use that knowledge to make decisions throughout the course, they'll appreciate how empowering this information is. Reinforce that this is a life-long process because we all change. Throughout the course, refer students back to their bull's eye chart as they discover something new about themselves. If they get into the habit of periodically reviewing these activities and updating their bull's eye charts and 10-year plans, they will be much more likely to stay on track with what is most important to them.

Career Choices was developed around the high tech/high touch theory championed in the best-selling book *Megatrends* in 1982. Before the onset of the personal computer, author John Naisbitt identified the coming technological revolution. He warned at the time that, along with the high tech options we were soon to have, we should not lose sight of the "high touch" all people need in their lives.

His phrase high tech/high touch illustrated the need to seek understanding and harmony between technology and human interaction. He believed that every application of technology needed to be offset with an equal application of human touch or interaction. He wrote that when high touch is ignored in implementing technology, technology encounters resistance.

The *Career Choices* curriculum and enhancements are built on the premise that brainpower is more valuable in the process of determining life-defining choices. The computer is a tool, not a crutch. To be truly successful in navigating the "slings and arrows" that life throws at us, we all need to be empowered to think on our feet and act or react appropriately and strategically. If we rely on computer-based surveys and personality tests to answer our most pressing questions about ourselves, we abdicate this most personal function.

By the end of Chapter 2, a marked difference can be seen in many of the students. Having a better understanding of themselves and their motivation is very empowering to students. They are about to learn that this is the first step to taking in guesswork out of making choices.

Chapter 3—*Lifestyles of the Satisfied and Happy: Keeping Your Balance and Perspective*

What comes first, career choice or lifestyle choice? Which did you choose first? Did your career dictate your lifestyle?

Taking a look at the different components of lifestyle, students start reviewing in general terms what decisions need to be made. This sets the stage for discoveries and choices made later in the course.

Students make their first attempt at writing their own mission statement, articulating how they want to be remembered. They will come back to this activity throughout the course.

Using a modified version of Maslow's hierarchy of needs, students experience a variety of issues that can impact their lifestyle and career choices. Using this model helps determine if their life is out of balance, a far too common problem in today's fast-paced world. Once an imbalance is identified, they're empowered to make the choices to get back on track.

Chapter 4—*What Cost this Lifestyle? Every Career Choice Involves Sacrifices and Rewards*

In this chapter, students explore three different lifestyle costs: the financial costs, the emotional and psychological costs, and, finally, the commitment costs.

For over 20 years, the budget exercise has been one of the most powerful activities of this curriculum. Students plan a budget for the lifestyle they envision for themselves at age 29. The resulting figure provides another important piece of data as they plan their future. They now have a quantitative checkpoint for determining what level of commitment they want to make to their education.

You'll want to spend time working through each budget line item. The more these numbers reflect the student's vision of their future lifestyle, the more believable their total budget figure is to them. The number they come up with as their budget total is critical to their decision-making process. It's an important figure when later, in Chapter 6, they start researching careers and the education each one requires. They soon discover that compensation is usually tied directly to education level.

Now that students have their ideal budget figures, they're ready to analyze a variety of budgets. The more comfortable they are with the budgeting process, the more they'll use it. As they continue through Chapter 4, they experiment with a "hard times" budget, budgets for a variety of family types, and the realities of living in poverty. However, money isn't everything, as the next activities point out. Students find case studies and activities exploring the psychological rewards and sacrifices any career and lifestyle might present.

The chapter wraps up by pointing out another cost of lifestyle: the importance of making a commitment. Using the commitment to education as an example, students apply math formulas and rubrics to explore in quantitative ways how the choices they make right now impact their future happiness and life satisfaction.

Chapter 5—*Your Ideal Career: There's More to Consider Than Just the Work*

NOTE: Because of the work your students have completed in the middle school coursework, they will already have a notion of the types of careers they might find satisfying. So by the time they get to a more thorough analysis of a particular career, they have an idea of which careers to study.

Through the various surveys, assessments, and activities in this chapter, students start describing their ideal career in general terms. By taking the assessments, they understand how broad those choices are. Students explore:

- Physical settings
- Working conditions
- Relationships at work
- Psychological rewards of working
- Mixing career and family
- Financial rewards
- Job skills

In addition, they explore concepts like flexible hours, composite careers, entrepreneurship, working virtually and telecommuting. By the time they complete the questionnaires, assessments, and surveys, they can write a description of a work situation that they would find personally pleasing and motivating.

Here's what students have learned so far from the beginning of the course:

- They have started articulating a future they find exciting and satisfying.
- They have a better understanding of who they are—their passions, work behavioral style, work values, etc.
- They have started defining a lifestyle they find pleasing.

- They have a notion of the economic, emotional, and commitment costs associated with that particular lifestyle.
- They have constructed a general description of their ideal working situation. Now they're ready to proceed to Chapter 6.

Chapter 6—*Career Research: Reading About Careers Isn't Enough*

After reviewing what they've learned about themselves in the first five chapters, students will conduct in-depth research on at least three careers they find appealing using a survey tool.

Just reading about and researching jobs using books and online resources isn't enough, though. After all: Tell me and I forget, show me and I remember, but involve me and I understand. The balance of this chapter presents activities that lead the student through more sophisticated ways of addressing the process of making a career choice. They envision what a day might be like in a particular job. You may also want to offer the option of shadowing someone at work.

In The Chemistry Test activity, students draw on what they learned about themselves in Chapter 2. Using information they have gained about their own personality and strengths, students learn the sophisticated concept of matching work behavioral styles to different careers.

It makes sense to reiterate that the ***Career Choices*** course is not just about choosing a career; it's about learning a process. On the other hand, it's important for students to become career-committed and career-focused. Studies show that entering college freshmen who have a specific career in mind are much more likely to complete/graduate on time.

Chapter 7—*Decision Making: How to Choose What's Best for You*

It's not the goal of this course to make a final career decision. After all, most people will have seven to ten different careers within their working life span. The goal is to help students create a vision of a future that they find appealing and, as a result, motivating. In the context of their 10-year plans, students are asked to focus their plan on one career area.

Be sure to remind them that this specific career choice will probably change at some point. By using the tools and strategies learned in this course, however, that decision-making process will be less stressful.

In Chapter 7, students are exposed incrementally to a systematic decision-making chart to help them with their career decisions and any other decisions they may make. Good decision-making is not instinctual; it takes knowledge, experience, and practice. Using the process, students learn a skill that will pay dividends in happiness and satisfaction throughout their lives.

Learning to determine and then articulate what we want is a complex yet very doable process. It is also critical to life satisfaction and success because, in the end, our lives are defined by the choices we make.

Chapter 8—*Setting Goals and Solving Problems: Skills for Successful Living*

This chapter opens with techniques for solving problems based on the writings of M. Scott Peck. For instance, the concept of delaying gratification is explored. As we know, for far too many people of all ages, the desire for instant gratification leads to trouble.

All good plans are quantitative, with measurable objectives that state what will be different, by how much or how many, and by when. In Chapter 8, students learn one of the most important skills of any planning process: how to write quantitative goals and objectives. They diagram goals and objectives to make sure each statement has all three components and, by the end of the chapter, they're able to write measurable objectives for their own lifestyle goals.

The goals and objectives they write are important. This is their first experience with creating an action plan, an empowering skill they'll use throughout the balance of the course and as they create their 10-year plan in Chapter 12.

Chapter 9—*Avoiding Detours and Roadblocks: The Road to Success is Dotted with Many Tempting Parking Places*

Life isn't easy and it isn't fair. Everyone, no matter how well they plan, faces barriers or problems at some time or another. How well they deal with these challenges determines how successful and therefore how happy they are in the long-term. You can do all the planning in the world, but if you hit a wall and can't get up, dust yourself off, and try again, you probably won't realize your most cherished goals.

The activities within this chapter help students explore and find strategies to address common problems that stymie people.

The chapter opens with a variety of exercises to assess and address self-limiting attitudes. The underlying message is that we all have to take responsibility for our own actions or, as the case may be, inactions. Using case studies, which are less threatening to students than discussing their own issues, they follow "friends" over a 15-year period and predict the outcomes based upon the effort and plans of each.

Students also look at the economic consequences of bad choices, whether it's dropping out of school or indulging in a bad habit. Using the magic of compounding interest, students determine the economics of a possible bad habit. They calculate how much they would have at retirement if they were to put their cigarette, designer coffee, or impulse shopping money in a retirement savings account instead. The result of not planning is shockingly illustrated in a monetary figure of huge proportions.

In Chapter 9, students look at the costs of self-limiting notions, whether it's about giving up a dream or feeling undeserving of success. A young person can be a bright individual, but if they aren't able to cope with the fears that are sure to surface during this transitional time in their lives, it's highly unlikely they're going to stretch themselves to get the education and experience they need to make it in today's world. Learning to overcome anxieties that limit their ability to move forward is an important skill set.

Let's face it. Some students don't have the benefits that go with being born into a family with the resources to give them a "leg up" in life. They may have little support and even less money. In this chapter, students create a 10-year plan for Yorik, a fictional character who has immigrated to the United States with nothing but his ambition. Starting with someone else's challenges helps make it less threatening when, in Chapter 12, they do the same for themselves.

Using the Career Alternatives chart, students are able to visualize various paths to career satisfaction. For instance, if they only have the resources to train to become a licensed vocational nurse, they can include strategies in their 10-year plan to move up the career ladder so they can realize their dream of being a registered nurse.

Students who work through these activities with your constant coaching and support are far less likely to be among those people who lament later in life, "If only someone would have told me what life was going to be like."

Chapter 10—*Attitude is Everything: Learning to Accentuate the Positive*

Success or failure is governed more by mental attitude than by mental capacity. If you think you can, you will. If you think you can't, you won't.

The best plans in the world can be sabotaged consciously or unconsciously by negative attitudes. Providing young people with the tools to evaluate, create, and maintain a positive attitude is critical to their future success in school and beyond.

In this chapter, students learn:

- How to use positive affirmations to push themselves to achieve cherished goals
- Strategies for achieving the highest standards of excellence
- Why a go-for-it attitude is critical to success
- How to recognize and reward a strong work ethic
- How to incorporate the skills and attitudes valued in the 21st century workplace
- Strategies for managing change

For many of your students, positive attitudinal shifts will be an important part of their growth process. The activities and exercises presented in this chapter will nudge them toward a more empowered mindset.

Chapter 11—*Getting Experience: Finding your first job*

In this chapter, students are exposed to the initial steps and strategies for getting a job. Students will be encouraged to find a beginning job in a field in which they are interested, even if it just means running errands or staffing the coffee cart. This provides an opportunity to be exposed to and experience the realities of work in their chosen industry. Most important, their experiences come at a time when students may still be able to make "course corrections" related to their education. For many, an entry-level job is also a powerful example of why further education is desirable. They'll see that jobs that require more education provide better rewards, both monetary and psychological.

Chapter 12—*Where Do You Go from Here? Writing Your 10-year Plan*

In Chapter 12, students take the data and insights they've gained in the course and put it all together for their 10-year plans.

Once the students complete Chapter 12, they enter the appropriate information from their ***Career Choices*** workbooks on My10yearPlan.com®. The online program then generates a summary of their 10-year plan and makes the information available to them for updating throughout high school.

When individuals are in the habit of evaluating who they are, what they want, and how to get it, particularly when making life's major decisions, the likelihood of long-term happiness and satisfaction is much higher.

Career Choices and Changes:
The College Version of *Career Choices*

Many districts have arrangements with their local community college or university for dual credit, usually in the form of dual enrollment or articulation. If your high school has this opportunity, your students will probably be using the college edition, Career Choices and Changes. *It is similar, following the same process of discovering who am I, what do I want and how to I get it, but with these differences:*

Career Choices and Changes brings the same self-discovery process found in ***Career Choices*** to a more mature audience: college students, people re-entering the workforce, individuals changing careers—anyone wrestling with the important questions of identity, life satisfaction, and future planning.

Career Choices and Changes covers all the topics in ***Career Choices*** but is written for a more mature audience with age-appropriate stories and examples. ***Career Choices and Changes*** also includes three additional chapters and expanded content in the last chapters.

What are the differences between **Career Choices** *(high school) and* **Career Choices and Changes** *(college)?*

Chapters 1 to 10 are nearly identical, because the decision-making process to that point is ageless and, therefore, the same. With the additional three chapters (Chapters 11, 12, and 13) and the expanded last two chapters, ***Career Choices and Changes*** is 100 pages longer than ***Career Choices***.

Chapter 11: Your Skills Inventory: The Precursor for Your Education Plan

Chapter 12: Study Skills for the Life-Long Learner: Developing Your Learning Plans

Chapter 13: Making Changes: The Inevitable Process

Chapter 14: Beginning the Job Search: Just Do It

Chapter 15: Where Do You Go from Here? Writing Your 10-year Action Plan

This last third of the college textbook emphasizes the development of a detailed Education Plan that is skills based, promoting not only traditional classroom learning but also the wide range of learning opportunities available.

In addition, ***Career Choices and Changes*** was designed to be used with My10yearPlan.com® Interactive.

An Introduction to My10yearPlan.com®

Personalization has been shown to be one of the most successful reform efforts in education today. How can we personalize education for all of our students and, in the process, help them develop a vision of a productive and attainable future? How can we act as advisors, using their dreams and plans to guide them to the greatest academic and personal success?

My10yearPlan.com® provides an online planning area where students can store, update, and save the data related to the development of their 10-year plans. When students share these plans, instructors and counselors are better equipped to advise students on their educational paths and provide support when academic effort doesn't match lifestyle aspirations.

Your students may be curious about this online program, because during the middle school course work they be introduced to this process. In that event, you may want to start with this basic introduction.

How Does It Work?

It starts with the ***Career Choices*** text. As students work through the book sequentially, gathering the data and developing the understanding required for their 10-year plans, they go online, log into their own password-protected area of My10yearPlan.com®, and enter the information they've collected about themselves. The My10yearPlan.com® input pages mirror ***Career Choices***, providing fields to hold all the information required for building their personal portfolio, Skills Inventory, and 10-year education and career plan online. This can be done in a school computer lab, in the library, or at home.

My10yearPlan Essentials

My10yearPlan Essentials provides a personal area online for students to store, review, and update their answers to the 25 keystone ***Career Choices*** activities that make up the 10-year plan. Once the learner inputs the information completed in ***Career Choices***, the My10yearPlan.com® system uses it to create a My 10-year Plan Summary Page. This overview provides a snapshot of the key goals and plans the learner has set for their education, finances, and lifestyle choices over the next decade.

By putting the essential artifacts from the planning process online, the learner also has the core pieces of their 10-year plan in a digital format that can streamline the process of compiling, editing, and producing a career portfolio.

My10yearPlan Interactive

The level of access available with My10yearPlan Interactive takes the digital planning experience a step further by providing an online home for ALL of the activities in ***Career Choices***. Each step of the learner's own unique self-discovery, decision-making, and personal planning process is outlined in My10yearPlan Interactive, so they have a complete, mobile record of who they are, what they want, and how they plan to get it.

My10yearPlan Interactive is more than just an electronic rendering of the planning process outlined in ***Career Choices***. It is a comprehensive, Internet-based system delivering over 100 exercises, activities, and surveys with which the learner interacts, facilitating a decision-making process that culminates in the development of a personalized 10-year plan that is not only quantitative but, more important, meaningful.

My10yearPlan Interactive is not a canned, one-size-fits-all experience where the learner has little control over or relationship with the outcome. Unlike those resources found on the web sites of the U.S. Department of Labor and commercial providers, My10yearPlan Interactive gives the computer a role that reaches beyond that of "tool" to something more akin to that of a coach, counselor, or mentor. The system gently guides, prompts, and, where necessary, prods the student through an in-depth decision-making process that often cannot be accomplished without this intense support.

Section 3

Course Options: Determining Your Course Structure

Course Options: An Overview

As you have probably already surmised, this program can be anywhere from 45 class sessions in length (using only the activities in the 12 chapters of the workbook, no extensions) to a complete semester course (the 12 lessons, in depth, plus one or both long-term projects). With the optional academic enhancements, you could develop a robust and rigorous year-long interdisciplinary course.

Time?

Your first consideration is to determine the amount of time you have to devote to this material. That will dictate which of the following pacing guide strategies to start with.

Once you've determined how much time you have (45 class sessions, 60 class sessions, a whole semester with 90 class sessions, or yearlong course), choose the appropriate model from the following suggestions.

As you'll see when you review the workbook, the scope and sequence of the delivery of the material is vital. Therefore you don't want to skip around but instead present the activities in order. Topics covered in earlier chapters will be expanded upon in later chapters.

Note: If you only have time for between 10 class sessions and 20 class sessions you may want to follow the coursework outlined in the abridged version of *the Instructor's Guide for a Middle School Bridge Program,* which outlines a reduced process and does not include a student workbook. You can order a copy of that instructor's guide by calling Academic Innovations' customer service team at (800) 967-8016.

Project-based Learning

Project-based learning is a student-centered method of teaching in which students are encouraged to think their way through complex problems or situations. In project-based learning, the instructor acts more as a facilitator. They help individuals or teams work their way through and eventually solve the problem or create a product. The instructor provides the students with a problem to solve or a product to create, but it is up to the students to discern what they already know, what they need to know, and how they will find the new information.

Overall, project-based learning is a superior method of both teaching and learning that demands of the students a higher degree of participation, cooperation, and development of critical-thinking skills. Because it is primarily self-directed, students take a much more active role in their own education and are typically more motivated to learn.

The ***Building a Bridge to Your Future*** coursework is a series a project-based learning opportuinites. The resources contained in this ***Instructor's Guide*** will help you develop these higher-order teaching strategies.

Learning Context

Learning in context provides the meaning and the in-depth understanding of a concept, information, or skill that an individual is required to learn. Learning in context is what bridges the gap between the abstract learning of the classroom and the practical applications outside of formal education.

When you integrate any or all of the enhancements to the ***Building a Bridge to Your Future*** curriculum, you'll provide a powerful opportunity for students to learn academic skills or technological applications in context.

What was once delivered through "drill and skill" will take on new meaning when layered into a ***Building a Bridge to Your Future*** course, because the information has been repackaged in the thematic format of self- discovery and personal planning.

Why it works is very simple. ***Building a Bridge to Your Future*** addresses the individual reader. By teaching self-knowledge along with reading, writing, and math, ***Building a Bridge to Your Future*** adds the context that makes basic skills relevant and motivates students to learn. Students are willing to pay attention, to work harder, to stretch themselves because, suddenly, what's going on in the classroom is of urgent personal interest.

Sample Pacing Strategies for *Building a Bridge to Your Future*

Your mission: Create a detailed, session-by-session lesson plan pacing guide that is easily managed.

Let's begin with the end in mind. You need to develop a customized, day-by-day lesson plan pacing guide that:

- Fits the parameters of your course time allotment
- Follows the scope and sequence of the middle school bridge curriculum—starting with Chapter 1 and working through to Chapter 12
- Culminates with each student developing their plan for their next steps as they transition into high school and beyond.

For Pacing Guide Strategies, see Section 6.

Pacing Guide for a Quarter Course 45 hours

A minimum of 45 hours is suggested for completing the work included in the student workbook.

A sample draft pacing guide will be available by late winter on the Teachers' Lounge and may be downloaded in a spreadsheet format. This format will make your job easier as you finalize your pacing. If you are familiar with the basics of working with a spreadsheet, you can readily add, update, or expand on the lessons.

You'll see that all of the activities in the workbook are included here, with suggestions on what combination could be covered in a standard class session of 50 to 55 minutes.

Once you have downloaded the basic 45-hour pacing guide, you can customize it using some of the following suggestions.

Pacing Strategies for a Semester Course

Each of the activities includes a variety of suggestions for extension and enhancements that you may have time to incorporate into your coursework if you have 90 hours (a semester) of class time. Once you study the lessons suggestions in this instructor's manual you can expand your course to include these additions. During your planning stage you'll want to detail what those expanded plans are in the column titled Lesson Enhancements.

And if the muse strikes, you may come up with additional ideas that can be used to meet the learning objective. Include those ideas on your pacing plan, providing as much detail as possible so later in the course as you are executing your plan, you have your ideas right there.

Expand your course by integrating the English Language Arts project.

But instead of just talking about how to find the best book, actually allow students to find a book about either one of the passions they listed or the career that is most intriguing right now. They will purchase the book, read it, and practicing the study skills of self-directed learner, read deeply and then report out on what they learned. See page 4/120 for details.

This is best delivered over the span of a semester course in order to allow students to research, read and reflect on the book they've chosen.

Semester course: 18 weeks	Outline of content
Weeks 1 through 3	Complete activities in chapters 1 thru 4 including all the extensions
Week 4 *This lesson will be based on the information from Chapter 11. This one time it is okay to go out of order. This is necessary to give your students time to research their book, order it, read it and create the final presentation project.*	Project # 1: Learning how to use Amazon.com to find the best book on a topic they're passionate about. Then students research a book about one of their identified passions, and place an order for that book.
Weeks 5 through 15	While students are waiting for their ordered books to arrive, you continue with the lessons chapters 5 on. Once students have their books, one day a week you all stop and read their chosen book, completing the reflective questions at the end of each chapter.
Weeks 16 through 18	During the last three weeks of the course, have each student make a presentation on what they learned reading their book. Encourage creativity as well as use of technical skills such as PowerPoints or even video. Presentation Skills—Lessons and practice on how to make an effective presentation. Include instruction on how to use digital resources within their presentations. Invite the three or four best presenters/presentations to present in front of the school board or to a community based organization such as Rotary or Soroptomists.

Optional: Expand your course by integrating real-world math using Lifestyle Math.

Once way to expand the material to a semester or year-long course would be to include the optional *Lifestyle Math*. For more information see pages 3/16 to 3/21 of this manual.

For example, for the first 45 to 60 hours of the course, students complete, under your tutelage, their work in their ***Building a Bridge to Your Future** workbook*. Then for the last portion of the course (30 to 45 hours) they complete their work in their *Lifestyle Math* workbook.

The budget exercise in high school is probably one of the most impactful activities of the whole ***Career Choices*** curriculum. Over the years, when we query instructors on theirs and their student's favorite and most motivational activity, it is the budget exercise. *Lifestyle Math* takes this project to a new level.

It is a 100-page math problem, using the math required for 8th grade competency, so you'll want to take a look at this option. See details beginning on page 4/125 to 4/128 of this manual.

Most high schools don't have time to incorporate this supplemental material but be sure to check first, as you won't want to include this if the high school is already doing it. But this is a good argument to doing this coursework in 8th grade. If your students transition into high school with this experience, their motivation to succeed will carry weight in a concrete number…the cost of their future lifestyle and the corresponding income their need to earn to meet that lifestyle. They'll understand that in most cases ***the more you learn, the more you earn***.

Pacing Strategies for a Yearlong Course

By combining the work in the middle school workbook with both the math enhancement and the English Language Arts described on pages 4/119 to 4/130, you can easily create a dynamic high school bridge program as well as an interdisciplinary course. Your students will be able to learn and practice sophisticated concepts, practice their math and English as well as exploring what makes them unique.

If you choose to create a year-long course from this material, you will able to "double dose" your students with high quality English and math assignments that meet the Common Core State Standards . This "new" course would support what your English and math instructors are doing academically.

The course instructor for this middle school bridge class will need to be comfortable teaching both English and math. This is within the reach of most middle school instructors, because the math required to teach *Lifestyle Math* is the math used in most people's everyday life; addition, subtraction, multiplication and division of whole numbers, fractions and decimals, along with simple algebra and statistics.

With careful planning you'll have a fast paced course where no one (especially you!) will be bored. Your students will quickly understand that this course is all about them. And for the early adolescents that is their key developmental task: identity formation and consolidation.

Upon completion of this coursework, students will be exposed to real world applications for both English and math. Additionally, their reading and math work will offer an opportunity to present instruction and provide practice in both study skills and presentation skills. For entering high school freshmen, these are vital for student success. Why? Because they'll arrive on their high school campus with an understanding of what their next steps should be in order to become both emotionally and financially self-sufficient adults.

What is the bottom line?

By the time students complete this coursework, not only will they be exposed to additional English and math skills but they will also, most importantly, understand the value of education—which will create the intrinsic motivation to succeed in both high school and post-secondary educational settings.

- Upon completion of their *Lifestyle Math* budget, once students have reviewed the salaries of careers that will provide the funds required for their envisioned lifestyle, they will understand that they have to work hard in school to attain a job that will support their family.
- Personalized learning is achieved when students read a book about one of their identified passions or the career they are most intrigued with. Because the content is of great interest to them, they will be motivated to go "deeper" into the content, which is what the Common Core standards espouse. This is known as "close reading." Instructors have the opportunity to not only help improve students' reading and writing skills, but to also infuse lessons about study skills and presentation skills in this context.
- When classroom material is about the student's interest and their future, you'll find their work increases in both quality and quantity. When students experience this level of success, it will give them the confidence and the experience to translate that to their academic work in high school.

If your school is interested in creating a standards-based, course for your students that gets them academically and emotionally ready for their decade of transition (high school, post-secondary, and career), please contact us at (800) 967-8016 and we will share with you this course outline in detail, along with a pacing guide with recommendations.

Other Options for Delivering the Coursework in the Workbook

Pacing Strategies for 25- to 30-minute Daily Advisories

As you go through both the student workbook and chapter four of this Instructor's manual, you'll note most of the individual activities could be completed in a 25 to 30 minute time span. If you school has a daily advisory period in which the bell schedule has been adjusted to include this educational strategy, you can use the workbook as a foundation material for your daily advisory periods, completing most activities in each session.

Pacing Strategies for Summer School Bridge Programs 3 to 4 hours per day over 3 to 4 weeks

If you follow the 45-hour pacing recommendations beginning on page 3/5, you'll see that you can easily complete the course work during a summer school session of three to four weeks that includes 3 to 4 hours per day of work devoted to the course content. During a summer session you'll want to include as many of the energizer type enhancements as possible. For that reason, you'll want to develop lessons for a total of 60 hours.

Integrating the Course Material into an Academic Class

Pacing strategies for class sessions over a full school year

If you are an English Languages Arts instructor, you'll quickly see how the work in the course can easily support your standards and your academic goals for your students. Integrating the coursework throughout your school year for two lessons per week, you can build a course that helps students learn English Language Arts content in context. For instance if you deliver these lessons, woven throughout the year, they would constitute 45 class sessions out of your total 180 hour sessions (on average).

You might want to do this throughout the year (say one or two per week) or batch them all during the third quarter or last quarter of the year.

Integrating the course material over a variety of disciplines

Share the different curriculum pieces with the other academic instructors on your campus, particularly those you know are innovators and pioneers. They are sure to find a variety of ways to integrate their work with your course work. Consider holding a meeting of these select academic instructors to share what you are doing and solicit their advice and their help.

As the content from your course starts impacting their students and they see the metamorphic changes to what were once insecure and unfocused teens, you'll recruit more champions who want to work together to support this project. Therefore keeping your whole school informed with what you are doing is vital. See Section 5 for buy-in strategies.

Pacing Strategies for Splitting the Coursework across 7th and 8th Grade

The course work can also be divided so the first **four chapters** of the workbook are presented in the seventh grade, and the last eight chapters are presented in the eighth grade.

If you choose this strategy here are a couple of key points to address:

Planning Strategies

- It is important that the instructors in the seventh and eighth grades have the same motivation to deliver the course material in a consistent manner, or otherwise the students will lose the scope and sequence of the material.
- Both teams should meet together to finalize a pacing guide for both grades. That would assure consistency of delivery.

Implementation Strategies

- Collect each student's consumable workbooks at the end of the 7th grade course work and keep them for the next year. That way important work will not be lost.
- Using their workbook, review the work done in the seventh grade prior beginning their work in the eighth grade.
- You might want to start with the students reviewing their work and writing an essay about what they learned about themselves in their 7th grade course.

The Abridged Version of the Middle School Program

If you do not have 45 hours to devote to completing the work in the student workbook there is an abridged program that can be accomplished in as little as 10 class sessions. For more information, call (800) 967-8016 and your Educational Consultant can provide details.

Instructor's Guide for a
Middle School Bridge Program
Developing the
Skills and Intrinsic Motivation
to Succeed in High School,
Post-secondary Education,
and the Workforce
An optional curriculum component of the
Get Focused...Stay Focused!™ Initiative
By Mindy Bingham

Integrating Academics into your Middle School Bridge Program

There is an optional academic textbooks:

- ***Lifestyle Math: Your Financial Planning Portfolio***

Lifestyle Math is a consumable workbook outlining a 100-page math problem that asks students to create a budget for the life they want when they are 29 years old. Students use real-life formulas, problems, and data to work personalized computations that cover each of the Common Core State Standards for Mathematical Practice:

1. Make sense of problems and persevere in solving them.
2. Reason abstractly and quantitatively.
3. Construct viable arguments and critique the reasoning of others.
4. Model with mathematics.
5. Use appropriate tools strategically.
6. Attend to precision.
7. Look for and make use of structure.
8. Look for and express regularity in repeated reasoning.

Because the math exercises are relevant to their lives, motivation and learning increase. For instance, once students have a figure for the cost of the future lifestyle they envision, they are asked to find a career that will support that lifestyle. Education suddenly takes on new meaning because students understand the need to apply themselves to their academic endeavors.

There are also dynamic online enhancements available, including LifestyleMath.com CareerChoices.com My10yearPlan.com®

LifestyleMath.com, the online correction tool for the ***Lifestyle Math*** workbook, uses technology to make personalized math possible. As students develop a budget for the lifestyle designed in their ***Lifestyle Math*** workbooks, they can check their individual math computations using this web-based instrument. Developed to support the learner, the program identifies where and when mistakes are made, directing students to retry their calculations. This immediate feedback should increase the learning that takes place by encouraging students to use their own brainpower to correct the error rather than giving them the answer.

Lifestyle Math: A Math Curriculum Option

As you design your course, you'll want to decide how and where you are going to incorporate ***Lifestyle Math*** and LifestyleMath.com.

Where to Incorporate Lifestyle Math

Lifestyle Math is most commonly used as a supplementary module in a math course. It can now be used as an interdisciplinary unit within a ***Building a Bridge to Your Future*** class.

While you may look to the math department for support, this part of the ***Building a Bridge to Your Future*** curriculum can be taught by any enthusiastic instructor who has good math skills and enjoys personal finance.

Programs can easily and efficiently incorporate ***Lifestyle Math*** into their year-long ***Building a Bridge to Your Future*** course. If you need more information than what's provided in this section of this instructor's guide, contact the Curriculum and Technical Support team at Academic Innovations at (800) 967-8016 for additional suggestions on integrating ***Lifestyle Math*** into your ***Building a Bridge to Your Future*** course.

If you are working with an interdisciplinary team or in an academy setting, the math instructor on your team could infuse ***Lifestyle Math*** into their lesson plans.

If your math department chooses to use ***Lifestyle Math*** as a supplemental activity to support your ***Building a Bridge to Your Future*** course, students at all math levels will benefit.

- For pre-algebra students, the review of basic math skills will be valuable, as will the application of math concepts related to their daily lives. This project-based math activity can be incorporated into the school year over 20 to 40 sessions.
- For algebra or higher-level students, integrate into your course with ***Lifestyle Math*** to expose students to a variety of ways math is used in daily life. This one activity will help increase their motivation to work harder in their traditional math course as the important role math will play in making life choices will become abundantly clear to them.
- You may use ***Lifestyle Math*** as an incentive, allowing time for students to work on their budgets once they finish other work. Students with solid basic math skills will view this project as a reward.
- For high-achieving students, you may provide ***Lifestyle Math*** as an independent study project. Students could come together periodically to share their insights and figures. Encourage these students to focus on STEM (science, technology, engineering, and math) careers, pointing out how these careers usually pay salaries that allow for more choices in lifestyle.

If working with instructors from another department, you'll want to share information about student progress, detailing what is giving them trouble or what topics are most appealing to them.

As you thumb through your ***Lifestyle Math*** workbook, you'll see a variety of energizers, project-based activities, and group brainstorming problems. These activities provide opportunities to differentiate instruction for students with a variety of learning styles. And, because these problems and case studies relate to their own personal issues, the activities effectively demonstrate how numeracy, financial literacy, and solid math skills can be used to craft a life of their choosing.

The personal planning process required to effectively plan for their future by factoring the costs of the lifestyle they envision is one of the most complex "problems" adolescents and young adults face.

As they research, write, and calculate, students are actively engaged in critical, creative, and strategic thinking challenges related to a topic of utmost importance: their future happiness. These lessons offer a variety of opportunities for collaboration, communication, and authentic assessment of their findings and plans.

Using the *optional* LifestyleMath.com will contribute a valuable new dimension to your course. The project-based learning experience provides content and critical thinking. If you utilize LifestyleMath.com to check calculations, you enhance computer skills as students build their math competency. Better yet, it exposes students to the types of real-world tools and calculators they can use online throughout their lives—even once they leave your campus.

To order a copy of *Lifestyle Math*, call (800) 967-8016 and speak with your Educational Consultant.

LifestyleMath.com: The Online Correction Key

Because of the individualized nature of the *Lifestyle Math* workbook, correction and assessment can be challenging. To help make that task as easy as possible, we've created an *optional* technology component to advise students on their computations.

LifestyleMath.com is made up of 47 mathematical problems and activities from the *Lifestyle Math* workbook. Until now, math problems from traditional coursework needed to be uniformly designed with one answer for each problem. Instructors would check student work against a written answer key. This limits math to answering "someone else's" problem. That's not very interesting for the average student.

This web-based tool allows students to quickly correct their own personalized math computations from their *Lifestyle Math* workbook. It personalizes mathematics by allowing students to dictate the variables used in their own calculations, giving the work they are doing more personal meaning. LifestyleMath.com makes correcting that work quick and easy, sparing teachers the sizable task of poring over each student's unique calculations and answers.

LifestyleMath.com embodies the dream of effortless correction, delivering a quick and easy tool for students to use at school or at home. After completing their computations the old-fashioned way (with paper and pencil in their workbook), students then go online with their password and check their answers digitally. Using the online correcting tool, students are alerted to any errors and encouraged to rework their computations. Once students arrive at the correct solution, they can print out their work and turn it in to you for credit.

An Easy and Intuitive Online Correction Tool

An example:

One student in your class may choose a home in another part of the country for $280,000, while another may choose to purchase a two-bedroom condo near their hometown for $185,000.Each student's math calculations and answers relating to the mortgage payments, interest, and utilities will be very different. The LifestyleMath.com online correction tool delivers a straightforward and simple way to check answers at school or at home—anywhere there is an Internet connection.

Here's how LifestyleMath.com works!

Students begin by working through a mathematical problem in their workbook the old fashioned way, with pencil, paper, and their own brainpower.

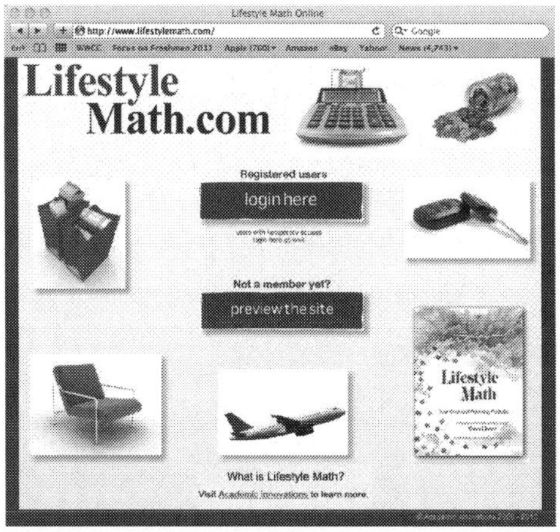

Once students factor each budget line item, they can go online to **www.lifestylemath.com** and login using your school's access information.

They'll choose the page they want to correct from the listing to access an online worksheet that looks like the page in their workbook.

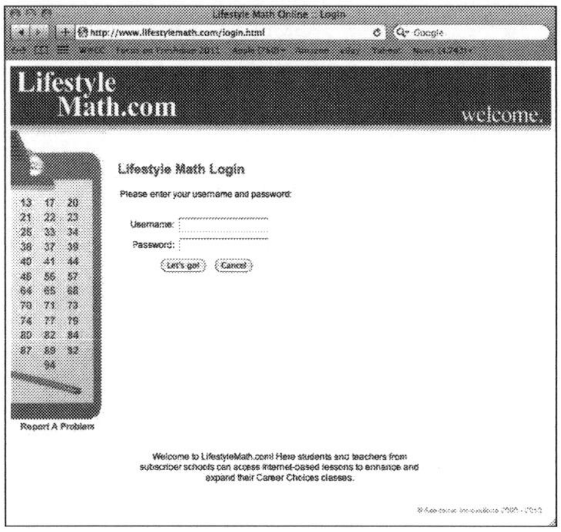

Students enter their own calculations in the appropriate fields and click "Check Answers!" The computer program reviews their work, notes any incorrect figures or incomplete information, and highlights it.

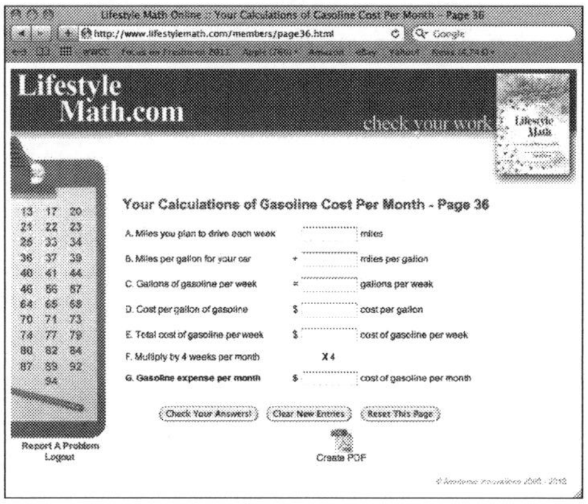

If the program finds inaccuracies, students can rework their mathematical calculations, go back online, and enter their amended figures. Once they successfully complete the assignment and all calculations are correct, they can print out their work and turn it in to their instructor for credit.

You'll find even reluctant math students are eager to pursue the correct answer because the final product—their budget—has meaning to them. What was once drill and drudgery will be attacked with newfound enthusiasm and curiosity. Students receive instant feedback on whether their mathematical calculations are correct. The end result of all this is confident students with increased career goals and, therefore, increased educational aspirations!

Lifestyle Math Contents

How to Integrate Lifestyle Math into Existing Math Courses

Recruit your math department to be part ofyour team. *Lifestyle Math* can be used as a supplemental activity for math classes at all levels.

Algebra: Students can use it for enrichment, perhaps as a bonus activity after a weekly quiz. This activity will reinforce the need for more advanced math classes while, at the same time, teaching important life formulas.

Pre-Algebra: Students can use it for supplemental activities to improve basic skills, increase problem solving and critical thinking, and demonstrate the importance of math. It will be motivational and therefore encourages students to continue with their math studies.

Basic Skills: Students can be motivated to focus on higher achievement by seeing how math relates to many other aspects of their lives. This workbook, with supplemental instruction on basic computation skills, could form the basis for a basic math course.

You may use *Lifestyle Math* as an incentive, allowing time for students to work on their budgets once they finish other work. Students with solid basic math skills will view this project as a reward.

For high-achieving students, you may provide *Lifestyle Math* as an independent study project. Students could come together periodically to share their insights and figures. Encourage these students to focus on STEM (science, technology, engineering and math) careers, pointing out how these careers usually pay salaries that allow for more choices in lifestyle.

Lifestyle Math is an important part of a semester-long program that provides double doses of both math and English.

Integrating Academics to Meet the Common Core State Standards

Because the Common Core focuses on the application of knowledge in authentic situations, teachers will need to employ instructional strategies that integrate critical and creative thinking, collaboration, problem-solving, research and inquiry, and presentation and demonstration skills.

— *Education Week*
Common Core State Standards Initiative mission statement.
Retrieved from www.corestandards.org 01/04/2013.

The Common Core State Standards Initiative, coordinated by the National Governors Association Center for Best Practices and the Council of Chief State School Officers, is an exciting step toward making sure students across the country graduate from high school prepared for college and workplace success.

By standardizing curriculum across state lines, students who relocate can more easily transition to academic life in a new school. These new standards also increase the depth with which students study certain topics, emphasize the use of more informational texts, and rely on additional cognitive skills, requiring less memorization and more analyzing.

And, above all, the Common Core State Standards are:

> *...designed to be robust and relevant to the real world, reflecting the knowledge and skills that our young people need for success in college and careers.1*

An overarching goal of the ***Career Choices*** series has always been to motivate students to apply themselves by helping them recognize the role academic skills play in their lives outside of the classroom. You could say ***Career Choices*** was delivering the Common Core State Standards long before they were common.

The lessons in the middle school workbook and this instructor's guide, supports the Common Core State Standards for English. You can find examples of how they address these standards throughout Section 4.

If you add to your middle school coursework the optional *Lifestyle Math* workbook, as students create a detailed budget, they encounter each of the Common Core State Standards for Mathematical Practice:

1. Make sense of problems and persevere in solving them.
2. Reason abstractly and quantitatively.
3. Construct viable arguments and critique the reasoning of others.
4. Model with mathematics.
5. Use appropriate tools strategically.
6. Attend to precision.
7. Look for and make use of structure.
8. Look for and express regularity in repeated reasoning.

Common Core State Standards for 8th Grade English

Depending on what depth you go into, this content will help you address the following Common Core State Standards for English:

Standards for Reading Informational Text

CCSS.ELA-LITERACY.RI.8.10

By the end of the year, read and comprehend literary nonfiction at the high end of grades 6–8 text complexity band independently and proficiently.

CCSS.ELA-LITERACY.RI.8.7

Evaluate the advantages and disadvantages of using different mediums (e.g. print or digital text, video, multimedia) to present a particular topic or idea.

CCSS.ELA-LITERACY.RI.8.8

Delineate and evaluate the argument and specific claims in a text, assessing whether the reasoning is sound and the evidence is relevant and sufficient: recognize when irrelevant evidence is introduced.

Standards for Writing

CCSS.ELA-LITERACY.W.8.2

Write informative/explanatory texts to examine a topic and convey ideas, concepts, and information through the selection, organization, and analysis of relevant content.

CCSS.ELA-LITERACY.W.8.7

Conduct short research projects to answer a question (including a self-generated question), drawing on several sources and generating additional related, focused questions that allow for multiple avenues of exploration.

CCSS.ELA-LITERACY.W.8.8

Gather relevant information from multiple print and digital sources, using search terms effectively; assess the credibility and accuracy of each source; and quote or paraphrase the data and conclusions of others while avoiding plagiarism and following a standard format for citation.

Standards for Speaking and Listening

(if students are doing presentations upon completion of their reading)

CCSS.ELA-LITERACY.SL.8.6

Integrate multimedia and visual displays into presentations to clarify information, strengthen claims and evidence

3/24

Section 4

Lesson Plan Suggestions for Each Activity

- This section contains suggested lesson plans for each activity in the workbook.
- We have provided more suggestions than you will likely have the time to implement, so take note of the ones you feel fit best with the main objectives of your particular course and your student population.
- Fit these lesson plans into the pacing guides you will develop using the information in Section 3.

These chapter-by-chapter, exercise-by-exercise classroom suggestions should be helpful as you develop your lesson plans. Each exercise has a learning objective with presentation suggestions. In addition, many outline optional activities, resources, and suggested reading and writing assignments.

Make notes about what works best with your students as you implement ideas, and please share your ideas. We would love to consider them for inclusion in a future version of this instructor's guide.

Vocabulary of Success

At the beginning of each chapter of the workbook there is a list of words used in that chapter. The vocabulary words will be helpful to students as they navigate high school, post-secondary education, and the world of work. Some of these words may be unfamiliar to students. It is important that they understand the definitions and meanings of these words before they begin reading the rest of the chapter.

Consider including a variety of activities to help your students learn these vocabulary words. They might include word search sheets, crosswords, Jeopardy-type competitions, etc. There are many free resources on the Internet that can be found simply by doing a search for "word games" or "printable word games."

Final Product

In the last chapter, the activity entitled *"Checkpoint: What Are My Next Steps?"* is one of the culminating activities in the workbook. Students will have already done some of the work of identifying areas they want to improve as they worked through the chapters and activities. This activity gives them an opportunity to put all of those ideas together in one place and to make a plan for their next steps—when they will do the work and who will support them.

Final Exam

Consider using this activity as part of your final grade. Giving this activity the importance associated with a final exam will encourage students to put in the time and energy this project requires.

Be sure to give plenty of time to do this work. It will require doing a review of all the work students have done so far. One strategy would be to introduce this activity as student begin the work in the workbook. Showing them what their final will entail and, as they work through the course material chapter by chapter, they can continually update their plan.

See page 8/3 of the manual and pages 165–167 of the workbook for more details.

Long-Term Projects

As we all know, project based learning is one of the best ways to learn. When important lessons and concepts can be infused into a project that has meaning for the students, more learning will be retained.

You'll want to consider one or both of the projects that start on page 4/117 of this manual as you develop your pacing guide and lesson plans for this course.

Chapter One
Introducing the 10-Year Planning Process

Chapter Learning Objective:

To introduce the 10-year planning concept and to motivate students to value the 10-year Plan they are going to create in high school.

The lessons in this chapter will provide a snapshot of what they are going to learn in this process and will get them excited about what they will learn about themselves in their freshman ***Career Choices*** course.

Preparing for this Chapter:

You may be asking yourself, "Why a 10-year Plan?" The easiest way to answer that question is to watch the short video found at: http://bit.ly/2d6FvwY

Designed for educators and parents, this video is a good resource to show at a parents' meeting or share the link in an email with the parents of the students in your class.

Begin with the End in Mind:

This middle school bridge program was designed to get students ready for the rigors and opportunities of high school. It is also the "on ramp" for the ***Career Choices***/My10yearPlan.com® work they will tackle on their high school campus. Therefore, it is important that you have a sense of the journey students are beginning.

For an overview of the *Get Focused...Stay Focused!* ™ program, watch the video at: http://bit.ly/2dCa0eM

Flipping the College Decision-making Paradigm:

Wondering why middle school students need to start career exploration? You may be thinking, "Isn't that what college/post-secondary work is all about, determining your career path?" Take a few minutes to watch the short video at: http://www.getfocusedstayfocused.org/flip

One of the goals of this chapter and the balance of the middle school bridge course is to help prepare students to be ready for this rigorous planning process when they matriculate to high school.

The 10-year Planning Process

Learning Objective:

To help students begin thinking about long-term planning, and to factor where they are in that process through self-evaluation.

Presentation Suggestions:

In a sense this is an assessment tool. Use this short essay to find out how much each student has thought about their future. You'll want to collect students' workbooks at the end of this chapter to evaluate this.

What you will probably discover is that most students haven't really thought much about what they will be doing in 10 years. Many haven't even fantasized about this. You may also discover that students who are strong academically are more likely to have considered what they want to be doing in the future.

Research supports the fact that students who enter college with an informed major/career path are twice as likely to graduate/complete as those that enter with the vague notion that college is the next step.

You probably don't want to give much instruction prior to making the writing assignment. Ask students to complete the assignment in class using the following directions:

In a quick-write format, respond to this question.

If you were asked what you would be doing in 10 years, what would your answer be?

Introduce students to a creative process used by many professional writers.

Ask students to close their eyes and think about that question. Allow three or four minutes of silent time to think about the question. After the time has elapsed, direct students to pick up their pen and write down their thoughts. Give them 10 to 15 minutes to respond to the question.

Activities:

Your students will probably have a mix of reactions—some have an idea of what they are interested in, some are completely lost, and some have pieces in place, but not a complete picture. It is important to emphasize that it is not expected that they will have done a lot of thinking about their futures at this point, and that this class will give them an opportunity to begin that process.

Once they have completed this activity, discuss these questions as a group:

- How many of you hadn't really thought about this?
- For those of you that have thought about this, how did you decide what you want to be doing?
- Are there any parts of your future plans that are unclear to you?
- Why would this be good to know?

How Ready are You to Think about Your Future?

Learning Objective:

To help students gauge where they are at right now with their feelings about planning for their futures and for the instructor to get a sense of each student's feelings about this process.

Presentation Suggestions:

Your students will complete this quiz individually. It will only take a couple of minutes. Emphasize that there are no right or wrong answers, this is just a quick survey to check how they feel when they think about their future. They are going to circle the response in each section that most closely matches their current state of mind.

Activity:

In pairs, have students discuss their responses. Then ask the class to think: If they scored 1 or 2 on each section, why do they feel positive, confident, and ready? If they scored 3 or 4 on each section, what do they feel they still need to figure out?

If students scored 1 or 2 on each section, they already have a future career in mind and may have even done some research. Great! This class and the class they will take in 9th grade with the ***Career Choices*** curriculum will help them to make sure that their choice will match their passions, personality, and future lifestyle goals.

It will also introduce them to the idea of having a "Plan B" in case their first career choice doesn't work out. Help them understand this concept by sharing a time in your past when you had a job in mind, but you also had a "Plan B" job.

For students who scored a 3 or 4 on these sections, this class and the class they will take in 9th grade with the ***Career Choices*** curriculum will help them to figure out their passions, personality, and future lifestyle goals.

Share the story of how you became a teacher. How did you figure out that you wanted to teach? What career goals did you have when you were your students' age? Was teaching your ideal career? If not, why did you change your mind? It's good for students to know that adults had to go through the same sort of career decision-making process they are going to be doing. If your career path was not straight into teaching or you didn't have a career class in middle school or high school, talk about how this kind of class might have been valuable for you and what it would have helped with.

What Will Your Life Look Like in 10 Years' Time?

Learning Objective:

To have students begin thinking in more detail about the many different possibilities for their futures.

Presentation Suggestions:

Deep Reading Strategy

Have a different student read each paragraph aloud, pausing at the end of each paragraph to discuss the content and to ponder some of the questions asked or points made in that paragraph.

"Deep reading" is required of self-directed learners, so this is a good skill for them to practice. Too often we skim text, much of it on screens, and we really don't stop to think about what the words are actually saying. Later in this course, students will learn the following process: research, read, reflect, recall.* By demonstrating reading and then reflecting in this activity, you'll start them on this process.

Don't mention what you are doing until you've completed reading and discussing the whole page. Then mention that they just completed a process of reading and recalling, one paragraph at a time. Ask how many students do this when they read text about a topic they are interested in?

Activity:

At the end of the page, have the students close their eyes and visualize what their futures look like. Give them two minutes to consider each prompt.

- Are you still taking classes/getting trained? In what?
- Will you be working for yourself or someone else?
- Which city/state/country will you be living in?
- Who will you be living with/spending a lot of time with?
- What kind of clubs/teams/other groups might you join in high school?

Note: This is the recall process—students are taking what they learned in their reading and applying it to their own experience or problem.

This process is also an example of the higher order thinking skills outlined in Bloom's Taxonomy: Analyzing, Evaluating, Creating. You'll want to use these strategies throughout the course, which has been designed to facilitate this for you and your students.

* More on this in Chapters 9, 10, and 11 as students learn techniques for becoming self-directed learners, the most highly-prized employees in the new economy.

Questions to Think About

Learning Objective:

To have students evaluate what they know and don't know about their future plans.

Presentation Suggestions:

Ask a student to read the paragraph at the top of the page aloud. Without further discussion, ask your students to write their responses in their workbooks.

Students will complete these prompts individually. They will need about 10 minutes. Emphasize that it is okay not to know the answer; this exercise is to help them figure out what they still need to think about.

Activity:

The last question:

What other questions or issues have you or your friends been thinking about that relate to your future?

Have students write one thing they have as a question about their future on a piece of paper. They will do this anonymously. Collect the pieces of paper and group them into 6 or 7 broad categories. You can either use the following categories or create unique categories based on your students' responses.

- Career
- College/Training
- Family
- Marriage
- Finances
- Physical Location/Housing
- Relationships
- Other

Draw a "Questions about the Future" mind map on the board covering the different topic areas your students have questions about.

You can do an Internet search for what mind maps look like if you haven't ever drawn one, but here are some basic directions:

Draw a circle in the middle of the board labeled "Questions about the Future." Next draw a branch from that circle for each of the six or seven main topic areas. Each branch should be a different color. Finally, draw smaller branches off each main topic area for the questions your students wrote down.

For example, one main branch or topic area might be college, and the smaller branches representing your students' questions might include: which college, which major, community college or university, paying for college, living away from home, etc.

Talk about how this course and the 9th grade ***Career Choices*** course will help them to figure these things out. Be enthusiastic about how fun it will be to answer all of these questions in these classes! Tell the students that they are beginning a voyage of self-discovery.

Strategies for Creating the Future You Envision for Yourself

Learning Objective:

Students will start exploring motivational triggers or cues. In this case, the cues will be words of wisdom that will help them focus on results.

Presentation Suggestions:

We all have short sayings or famous quotes that we use to trigger a response or push ourselves forward with confidence. There is a reason that the motivational poster industry does so well. We all appreciate these prompts to help us stay on track.

If you have a poster or saying that you particularly like, share it with your students. Explain a situation where that quick prompt has been helpful to you.

Activity:

Assign each quote to a different student to read aloud, finishing with the name of the person it is attributed to. Once the quotes have all been read, ask students to complete the questions on page 17 of the workbook.

As a class, review each quote. Ask those students who chose each quote to comment on what they thought the person meant, in what context they thought it was stated, and what attracted them to the quote.

Optional Energizers:

Print out each of the quotes and attach them to the wall around the classroom. Assign one student to each quote to read it out loud to the group. Have students stand next to the quote they like most, and explain why.

If there is access in class to a computer, the students could look for other quotes they like, using the search terms like "destiny quotes" or "fate quotes" or "future quotes."

Students may already have a favorite quote or they can make up a motivational quote of their own about their futures. They could design a poster around the quote, and these could be hung on the classroom walls.

Imagining My Future Life

Learning Objective:

To help students realize that the career, education and life decision-making process doesn't have to be onerous, but that it will require some thought, discussion, energy, and research.

Presentation Suggestions:

Students will revisit what they imagine their future life to look like, incorporating some of the new insights they have gained about future possibilities. After only a few activities to get students thinking about their future, they will be ready to try the essay from the beginning of the course again.

They should feel more successful this time, because they'll have more to write. And, as with everything in life, when we experience success, it is motivational for us to continue.

If you were asked what you would be doing in 10 years, what would your answer be?

This will be the same quick-write activity done at the beginning of the course. Repeat the creative process used earlier. However, this time enhance the process by asking them to review the work they've done in their workbooks so far first. Then ask them to close their eyes and think about the question. Allow three or four minutes of silent time to think about the question. After the time has elapsed, direct students to pick up their pen and write down their thoughts. Give them 10 to 15 minutes to respond to the question.

Activity:

After completing this second essay, have your students look back at how they responded to this question previously. Ask students to share with a partner what is different and what has changed since the first time they answered this question.

Now ask them to answer the questions below with their partner, considering what they wrote the first time and what the just wrote.

- Do you now have new ideas about what your future might look like?
- What are some of those new ideas?
- Do you have new questions about your future?
- What are some of those questions?

This is an opportunity to show the students how reflecting and discussing can give them new questions and new ideas. This is going to be how this curriculum and the processes they are learning works—the more questions they have, the more they will want to research the answers. The more they reflect on those answers, the more new ideas they will have about their futures.

My Lifestyle Choices

Learning Objective:

To familiarize students with some of the possible future lifestyle choices they will be making.

Presentation Suggestions:

Read or have a student read the paragraph at the top of the page aloud to the class.

Looking back at the essay they just wrote, have students check the box that reflects their thoughts on each of the topics.

Explain each concept to make sure that students fully understand each before they fill out the grid. The students may not understand topics such as the status of a chosen job, working conditions, or what types of benefits might be possible (i.e., medical, dental, vision, 401K plan, profit sharing, tuition reimbursement).

You will need to explain these concepts one at a time, and check for understanding before students mark the appropriate column.

You'll probably find that most students check "I didn't think about it" for many of the topics. Perhaps take survey of which questions have the most "I didn't think about it" responses.

So much discussion is centered on career choice that sometimes we don't look at how that choice impacts lifestyle choices. Assure your students that they will explore a variety of these topics in more depth in their high school program.

Activity:

As you read through each of the statements, it may become clear that students have relatively vague notions about certain topics. If you have internet access in class, ask students to search for some of these terms and then to write definitions in their own words. If access is not available in class, assign the definitions for homework. Students could access the internet at home or from the library, or they could choose to interview the adults in their families to find out what the terms mean to them.

Making a Career Choice
Who Am I? What Do I Want? How Do I Get It?

Learning Objective:

To introduce the career/life decision-making process—who am I, what do I want, and how do I get it?—they will learn in their freshman ***Career Choices*** course.

Presentation Suggestions:

Use the deep reading strategy learned on page 4/6 of this manual, perhaps discussing each section rather than each paragraph.

After students take turns reading and you have discussed the points or questions of each paragraph/section, they can complete the following activity.

Activity:

Who am I? What do I want? How do I get it?

Post these three questions in separate locations on the classroom walls. Ask students to take turns standing next to each question and offering one answer.

For example:

> Who am I? I am a quiet girl who likes art.
>
> What do I want? I want to become an architect.
>
> How do I get it? I will need to learn how to use a computer to design houses.

You'll probably want to model this activity by sharing your own responses to these questions.

Be sure to let your students know that this is a very quick overview of what they will study in much more detail when they develop their 10-year Plans in their freshman year.

Why Do I Need a 10-year Plan?

Learning Objective:

To help students understand why they need a 10-year Plan even when they are in middle school.

Presentation Suggestions:

This is a good question particularly when you are just becoming a teenager. 10 years is a long time.

Draw on your understanding of this topic using what you learned watching the videos on page 4/3.

Use the deep reading strategy for the content on page 4/6.

Motivational introduction video:

Show the video "Introduction to ***Career Choices***" hosted by Dain Blanton and available on The Teachers' Lounge or on My10yearPlan.com®. The video can also be found at this link: http://bit.ly/1tiW8pl

Your Online 10-year Plan

Learning Objective:

To introduce the final product of their freshman course: A meaningful and personalized 10-year Plan.

Begin with the end in mind—show students a sample 10-year Plan and introduce it as the type of product they will produce. Understanding what they are going to learn about themselves, not only in this course but throughout high school, should be motivational and eye opening. By this point in the course they are starting to learn the variety of topics they need to think about as they plan for a future of life satisfaction and happiness. This physical manifestation of that process will help solidify their understanding.

Presentation Suggestions:

Read the paragraphs that precede the sample. Ask students to study the sample plan on pages 24 to 27 of the workbook. This is a print out of a sample student's 10-year Plan Summary Page. Present this as an example of what your students' 10-year Plans will look like when they complete their freshman course.

Review the sections included in the plan (e.g., My Mission in Life, My Career Choice, etc.).

Activity:

Ask students to silently read Jordan's 10-year Plan Summary. Allow at least 10 minutes for this.

Now ask students to pair up and answer these questions together:

> What do you find most intriguing about Jordan?
>
> Does Jordan's plan look realistic? Why or why not?
>
> If you were Jordan's counselor, how helpful do you think this information would be? Why?

After the teams have had 10 to 15 minutes to discuss these points, bring everyone back together.

Poll the pairs the group by asking: "How many think the plan is realistic?"

Ask a few to comment on why they think the plan is realistic, and ask a few who disagree to comment on why they think Jordan's plan is unrealistic.

Work with the *Get Focused...Stay Focused!* ™ team at the high school to gain access to a demo My10yearPlan.com® account. Log in and show the different types of information involved in the 10-year Plan process.

- If the high school is using My10yearPlan.com® Essentials, show students a fictional student's ***10-year Plan Summary Page.***
- If the high school is using My10yearPlan.com® Interactive, provide a printed copy of a fictional student's ***My 10-year Plan and Portfolio*** in a three-ring binder.

Skills-based Education Plan

As your student's progress through high school, they will be creating a skills-based education plan rather than a traditional student education plan, which only outlines the courses needed to graduate. Not all skills required in the workplace can be learned in a classroom. This is a chance to introduce the many ways people can learn in today's world. A review of the second column provides examples of the variety of learning opportunities today.

For a better understanding about this, watch the short video, The Insufficient Degree: http://bit.ly/2dlxUcJ

Meant for educational leaders and parents, you might want to share this as well, with your peers and parents.

If your students enter a high school that has the *Get Focused...Stay Focused!* ™ program, their ***Career Choices*** freshman course will be followed by modules in the 10th 11th and 12th grade that will lead to a skills-based education plan. This will help to assure they will be prepared and competitive for a job in their chosen field.

Jordan's Plan

Learning Objective:

To build an understanding of how a 10-year Plan can be used.

Presentation Suggestions:

Through class discussion and brainstorming, answer the questions outlined in this activity.

Class Discussion:

Once the students have studied a copy of Jordan's 10-year Plan, conduct a class brainstorm.

How can these 10-year Plans be used?

Answer: Students can share these documents with advisors and counselors, teachers, close friends, parents, and mentors.

As a class or in small groups, brainstorm the following:

- How they could be shared?
- What kind of information would be learned from the 10-year Plan document?

Your Plan

Learning Objective:

To setting the stage for what is to come. To help students understand how a 10-year Plan can be used for their benefit as they plan a life that will match their aptitudes and goals.

Presentation Suggestions:

Remind your students that the first draft of their plans will be completed in 9th grade. If their school is a *Get Focused…Stay Focused!* ™ high school, they will be updating their plans in subsequent years as they continue their career exploration and post-secondary education planning process. You'll want to start encouraging them to think about periodically reviewing and updating their 10-year Plans—not only during high school—but *throughout their lives.*

The data, dreams, and goals in their 10-year Plans will come in handy when interviewing for college admission or a job. Someday they may even want to share their plan with their children.

You'll want to talk about their 10-year Plan with excitement and reverence, so your students understand the power this document will have in helping them envision and work toward the life that they'll find rewarding and satisfying.

Common Core State Standards for English

CCSS.ELA-LITERACY.SL 8.1 Engage effectively in a range of collaborative discussions (one-on-one, in groups and teacher led) with diverse partners on grade 8 topics, texts, and issues, building on others ideas and expressing their own clearly.

CCSS.ELA-LITERACY.CCRA.SL.2 Integrate and evaluate information presented in diverse media and formats, including visually, quantitatively, and orally.

Chapter Two

Student Success: Perseverance is as Important as Brain Power

Chapter Learning Objectives:

More and more research substantiates the fact that success in educational settings and in the workforce requires far more than mastery of academic skills. As important (if not more so) are what are commonly known (erroneously) as soft skills.

From this point forward, you'll note that the odd numbered chapters deal with career exploration topics and the even numbered chapters address issues related to social and emotional intelligence and character development. This format integrates these two important domains so the content can be learned in context.

In this chapter, students will:

- Develop an awareness of the need for delayed gratification
- Explore how much effort and perseverance they put into tasks
- Understand the concept of grit
- Learn about growth mindset
- Be able to explain how the brain changes through challenges
- Explore whether they have a fixed or growth mindset
- Strategize how to move towards a growth mindset

The Power of Thought: Challenges and Emotional Rewards

Learning Objective:

To help students learn that overcoming a challenge results in a greater emotional reward than doing something that comes easily to them. If students can see the benefit of this, they will be more open to tackling the challenges they will confront throughout their lives as they grow and learn.

Presentation Suggestions:

Open by reading the introduction and then sharing a personal story with your students of a time that was challenging for you. Share what you had to do to be successful and how you felt when you succeeded. Try to use multiple adjectives about how you felt. Share whether you felt persevering was worthwhile.

Make Notes Here:

Activity:

After you share a personal example, ask students to sit quietly and think about a situation in their own lives when they had to overcome a challenge. They will use this situation in the following activities, so allow ample time for them to come up with an example.

Ask students to describe the situation in writing in their workbook.

If some students are struggling to think of something, ask for three or four volunteers to share their example aloud in class. Those suggestions may trigger everyone's thinking.

Are some students still struggling? Here are some examples to trigger their thinking:

- Learning to swim, ride a bike, or play a sport
- Cleaning out your closet
- Completing a particularly difficult math problem or finishing a school project that you didn't really find interesting
- Getting up to speak in front of an audience
- Confronting a friend productively on a topic that otherwise would have ended a friendship or sitting with someone at lunch who had been wrongfully ostracized by others

Once you know that everyone has an example of a situation, have students identify the emotional rewards of tackling a difficult situation and following through.

The students will probably come up with additional vocabulary to express their emotions (possibly slang!). Write the words they came up with on the board to reinforce and validate their feelings.

After students enter their responses to the last two questions, ask volunteers to share these final thoughts. In most cases students will agree it was worth it to see a difficult task through.

Ask your students to think back to the beginning. Before they tackled the challenge, what was their energy level as a percentage? Compare that to the energy level they felt when they had persevered and succeeded.

- Did success make them feel energized?
- Did it give them the confidence to tackle subsequent challenges?
- How long did that feeling last?
- If it disappeared over time, how could they summon it again when tackling a new challenge?

Delayed Gratification

Learning Objective:

Students will understand the concepts of delayed gratification and instant gratification, and how delayed gratification leads to long-term success.

Presentation Suggestions:

There is a lot of research that shows us that the ability to delay gratification helps us to be successful in our future lives. Share with the students a time when you had to use delayed gratification instead of instant gratification to reap the benefits at a later point. It could be a story as simple as saving up for a car or a down payment on a house by giving up your expensive morning coffee or cable TV.

Make Notes Here:

- What was difficult for you in delaying gratification?
- How did you make yourself wait?

Using the challenging situation in the previous exercise, have your students complete the work in the workbook. If necessary, read the directions together.

Activity:

Write on the board the 2 terms "instant gratification" and "delayed gratification." Give an example of each, and ask the students to brainstorm some other examples.

Show the video "Don't eat the marshmallow yet" by Joachim De Posada on Ted Talks: https://www.ted.com/talks/joachim_de_posada_says_don_t_eat_the_marshmallow_yet?language=en

Class Discussion:

What are some strategies the students in the video used to delay gratification?

After the students answer the question, "What did you do to make yourself wait instead of going for a more instant, but probably less valuable reward?" put them in groups of three or four and ask them to share their techniques for delaying gratification.

Did students hear any ideas from other group members that they liked and might try in the future?

Have students write those ideas down in the bottom section of the page. Have them ask parents/guardians/other adults/older siblings for their ideas, too.

Effort and Perseverance

Learning Objective:

Students will understand that outcomes are determined by the amount of effort and the amount of time they are willing to put into a task, and will assess their own levels of effort and perseverance.

Presentation Suggestions:

Share with your students an example of a class you had to take that was really hard for you, that you were eventually very successful in, using the following topic outline:

- What was the class? Describe in detail what was expected.
- Why was it hard for you?
- How much effort did you put in to being successful, on a scale of 1–5, with 5 being a lot of effort?
- How hard was it for you to persevere to be successful, on a scale of 1–5, with 5 being very hard? Were you willing to put in the time to succeed? Did it take longer than others, for instance did you have to repeat the class?
- What would your total score be?
- What would that result mean?

Activity:

Students take the quiz for themselves.

In small groups, ask students to discuss:

- Are they happy with how much effort and perseverance they put into a challenging task they outlined earlier?

Grit

Learning Objective:

Students will learn about the concept of "grit" or "stick-to-itiveness."

Presentation Suggestions:

Research has proven that grit is a higher predictor for success than intelligence. This means that putting in effort to doing something, and persevering for as long as it takes to be successful, is the secret to success.

Show the video "The Key to Success – Grit?" by Angela Lee Duckworth on Ted Talks:

https://www.ted.com/talks/angela_lee_duckworth_the_key_to_success_grit?language=en

Class Discussion:

What was interesting/surprising to the class about the ideas in the video?

Ask students to write a definition of grit and then think of ideas to build their own grit.

What are some ideas they came up with?

Write those ideas on the board. Have them ask parents/guardians/other adults/older siblings for their ideas, too.

Staying the course, even if it takes more time.

In groups of two or three, have students discuss the following:

- Have they ever had to repeat a class or some other form of learning (like how to play tennis or master a computer program), because they were not able to grasp the concepts the first time and needed more time to understand the material? How did they feel about having to repeat the lessons? Did that stop them from mastering the material?

Come back together and ask individuals to share their experience. Try to find someone who quit because they didn't want to put in the time or they were embarrassed or they felt like a failure. Without shaming them, asked what they learned from that experience. That will be a discussion that will be important as you later talk about failure as a springboard.

Our Brains: How they Change and Our Abilities to Grow

Learning Objective:

Students will understand the science behind how our brains change in order to feel empowered to go for it and learn as much as they can, and not be hampered because they are "not smart enough."

Presentation Suggestions:

Too many students don't feel that they are smart (brain power). As a result, they "give up" and don't push themselves to learn. And while natural ability is important, it is not the key factor in their success.

Attitude (growth mindset) is just as important (and perhaps more important as research is showing) as aptitude (brain power). In Asian countries, students have been raised with the belief that it is not how smart you are but how hard you work. That expectation contributes to the documented higher levels of academic success of Asian students. So it is important for students, early in their educational journey, to embrace this reality.

This section is fairly scientific, but if students understand that their brains change through challenge, this will be important for their motivation. In simplistic terms, explain to your students the brain is like a muscle. As you would exercise your biceps to make them stronger, you need to exercise your brain to make it stronger.

Ask for volunteers to share their responses as to why they feel the way they do about their natural ability or brainpower. If you don't get someone to admit they don't feel as smart as other students don't push it. But by this time in their lives, most classmates know who the smart ones are and who is considered slower.

Discuss the information in the workbook.

Have the students read the explanation about mindsets in their workbook and how our brains change. You will need to explain some of the concepts and vocabulary in the section on neuroplasticity. It would be helpful to show them a diagram of a brain with dendrites and neurons—there are lots of images that come up if you search "neuroplasticity" on the Internet.

Ask students to share what they currently do to "exercise their brain."

Brainstorm what additional things you could do to strengthen your brain and write them on your classroom board. Some examples might be strategic video games that they play, or they may have a family member who does Sudoku.

Perhaps for the rest of the course as you open class you might want to say:

Good morning class! Are you ready to exercise and strengthen your brain?

Activity:

You can share with them a real life example of neuroplasticity helping to reduce the symptoms of Parkinson's disease.

Parkinson's disease afflicts about a million Americans—and that number is going up as the population ages. They face a gradual loss of control over their muscles, leading to tremors, loss of balance and difficulty walking or speaking. Exercise seems to promote neuroplasticity in people with Parkinson's disease; and this exercise-induced neuroplasticity is accompanied by behavioral recovery.

In a few parts of the country, boxing clubs are pioneering this technique. They are offering classes for people with Parkinson's disease. One trainer describes the effect on the brain when using boxing as a technique as being about pushing yourself past your limits and reaching that point that you don't think you can reach. He says that when you get that "runner's high," your neurons start clicking, you get new cells working, and everything works more effectively.

Show the video "Title Throws Parkinson's a 1–2 Punch,"

https://www.youtube.com/watch?v=EA6--Ms2uQ0

or Google "NBC4 News Title Boxing Newbury Park"

Class Discussion:

If people can retrain their brains to overcome symptoms of Parkinson's disease, what would the students want to retrain their brains to do?

Brain Power versus Growth Mindset

Learning Objective:

Students will assess their own mindset to evaluate whether they have a fixed or growth mindset.

Presentation Suggestions:

After discussing the information about Growth Mindsets, found in the workbook, have students take the Survey to determine if they have a growth mindset or fixed mindset. If they scored 1-7 points they have a fixed mindset, which they hopefully now want to change. If they scored 14-21 they have a growth mindset. If they score in the middle with 8-13 points, they can easily move towards a growth mindset.

Class Discussion:

Why is a growth mindset preferable in today's world?

Ask your class to think about adults they know and share stories of individuals who have either of the mindsets, (without sharing names).

Divide the class into triads (teams of three people) to discuss this case study.

Imagine that you are an employer and you are interviewing two people. During that process you determine through your questioning that one has a fixed mindset and one has a growth mindset. Which would you hire and why?

Bring the whole class back to share their thoughts on why they would hire someone with a growth mindset.

You may want to read:

Mindset: The New Psychology of Success
How We Can Learn to Fulfill Our Potential
by Carol S. Dweck, PhD (Ballantine Books, 2008)

Your Future Happiness

Learning Objective:

Students will start the process of identifying their long-term education or training goals, based on what they've learned about effort, perseverance, grit, delayed gratification and growth mindset. Ideally this quantifiable information will help all students see that their goals and dreams are attainable.

Presentation Suggestions:

You can model this for students by drawing your education/training path on the white board as a winding road.

- Draw a road with bends in it running from the bottom to the top of the board
- Write the highest level of education/training goal that you have achieved at the top of the road.
- Add some stages to the road – graduated high school, community college, teaching practice, degree etc.
- Draw some graphic representations of challenges that you faced – time, money, lack of family support, taking care of family members etc. and add them to the road map.
- Discuss which parts of the journey you had to put a lot of effort into. Circle them!
- Were there ever times when you thought you would not be successful? Put an exclamation point next to them!
- What do you wish you had known at the beginning of your journey that would have made it easier to believe that you would be successful?

Activity:

Have students draw a similar career path, projecting their future educational journey rather than looking back as you did.

Using this graphic as their guide, respond to the prompts in the workbook when thinking about their ambitious plan for education and training. This is an important assignment so give them time to complete it and then ask students to share their plans. For many it will be the first time they've been encouraged to dream beyond what their self-assessment or that the assessment of others is as to their talents.

Chapter Three
Know Thyself

Chapter Learning Objective:

To introduce the concept of "identity" and how understanding what drives us and then develop to a plan for realizing our dreams and goals is a process we all want to conscientiously pursue.

One of the key goals of the freshman transition course that students take when they enter high school is to help each student become aware of his or her own identity and ambitions and then to develop a 10-year action plan for realizing the goals that match their personality and aspirations.

This chapter helps students start to answer the question: Who Am I? The renowned psychologist, Erik Erikson, categorizes the development stage from 13 to 19 as the one for identify formation. This is the time, according to Erikson, when individuals become identity achieved. The existential question for this stage of life, according to Erikson is: Who am I and what can I be?

During this course you'll expose students to some basic concepts around those questions.

The activities in this chapter will prompt students to start thinking about who they are and the energy they want to expend to achieve an ideal future. It provides baseline information on how much thought students have given this topic, and whether their ambitions are relatively high or low.

The Real You

Learning Objective:

Students will begin to examine their characteristics, personality traits and strengths in order to articulate what makes them unique, and so that they can eventually find a career that will be a good match for them.

Presentation Suggestions:

Start the class by having students break into teams of four or five.

1. Within the team have one person be an interviewee applying for a job for a high school student at either a fast food restaurant or a retail clothing store. The team can decide which one.
2. Then they choose one volunteer to be the interviewee/job seeker. The others are a panel representing the interviewer/employer.
3. Ask the interviewee to respond to the one question: "Tell us about yourself."
4. Ask the interviewees how well they thought they did in the interview. What was hard for them?
5. Ask the interviewing teams what they heard that would make them want to hire that interviewee.

Their reasons for hiring someone will probably be based on how well the interviewee could talk about their strengths.

Now read the introduction in the workbook and ask the class members to complete the quick write assignment on that page.

Activity:

Ask the students to write down on a piece of paper, or in the margin of their workbook, 3 adjectives that they would use to describe you, their instructor. Then on the board write down the 3 adjectives you think best describe you.

- How many students used the same adjectives as you used to describe yourself?
- If you are feeling brave, ask them what other adjectives they used to describe you – tell them to keep it positive!

Discuss how people see us differently from how we see ourselves, and how some of who we are is hidden.

Use an iceberg analogy by drawing it on the board – with the parts of you everyone knows about above water (you like tennis, you have 2 children, you speak Spanish), and some of the hidden parts under water (you play ukulele, you make excellent pizza, you are afraid of heights, you love to read mysteries).

Activity:

Provide students with magazines to cut out items they feel represent them to make a collage, or have them draw a representation of different aspects of themselves on a sheet of paper or in the two pages provided in their workbook. They could use the iceberg analogy, or just design something that represents the whole of themselves.

Have them present their designs to the class, explaining them. These can be stuck onto the cover of their workbooks like a dust jacket or posted around the walls of the classroom.

For a real energizer, have student turn in their collages being careful not to share them with anyone in class. Then post them around the room, with no identification of who they are on the front, place a number below them and then give everyone a handout with numbers in the first column and names of students in alphabetical order in the second column. Give students 15 minutes to try to match the collage with the name of the person who created it. They can do this as individuals or as teams.

The person who gets the most right could give a "prize" that could be a simple as extra points on the next exam or assignment.

Discovering Who You Are

Learning Objective:

Students are introduced to a basic understanding of the breadth of their personal profile including their personality style, strengths, skills, talents, and values.

Presentation Suggestions:

Open the class by showing the video from the ***Career Choices*** course for Chapter Two:

Show the video "Chapter 2—Your Personal Profile" hosted by Dain Blanton and available on The Teachers' Lounge or on My10yearPlan.com® or at http://bit.ly/2dP2i4v.

This video will most succinctly present the topics that students will explore about themselves, not only in their freshman course but throughout their lives. Don't worry that they'll see it again in their freshman course. These are topics we could all review periodically throughout our lives.

Activity:

Have the students write what they learned from watching the video, and then discuss:

- What did they learn?
- What do they want to find out about themselves?
- How are they different now from 3 years ago when they were in elementary school?

You will want to reassure them that they will be changing a lot during their teens and early twenties, and that they are still in the process of developing. However they have some character traits and strengths that will stay pretty consistent throughout their lives. This curriculum and the subsequent courses in high school will allow them to spend time reflecting on who they are now, who they may become, strategies for growth and what vocation to follow.

Fame

Learning Objective:

Students will learn that the individuals who are famous possess qualities that they may want to emulate. They will consider how they would get skills, aptitudes and attitudes they think are desirable.

Presentation Suggestions:

After a brief introduction, have students first complete the activity prompts in this exercise.

Think, Rethink! Activity

Once they are done with their first draft, share with your students a picture of someone famous you would like to meet, from any time period. Talk about what that person accomplished, and what it is you admire in that person.

- Does that person have any skills, aptitudes or attitudes that you would like to develop? How would you develop them?
- Or did you already develop some of them? If so, how?

Now ask them to review what they've already written and enhance their initial comments with more ideas.

Activity:

Once students have re-edited their workbook, on the board/whiteboard create a two-column document/graphic. On the left hand side write down the names of the famous people your students would like to meet, and on the right hand side, the attributes they admire. Go around the room one at a time so students can share their person and one attribute. If more than one students identifies an individual add stars next their name.

Upon completion of this chart you should have an impressive list of attributes.

Discuss as a group how students could go about developing those attributes?

You may even want to make a poster of this chart to hang in your room.

Success

Learning Objective:

Students will start to identify what it means to be successful and how they would define success for themselves.

Presentation Suggestions:

In preparation for the activity in the workbook, have students write down the name of someone they think is successful. It doesn't have to be a famous person. It could be someone like a family member, friend, or someone like a teacher or neighbor that they know personally.

- How would they describe that person?
- In what ways do they think that person is successful?
- Are they hearing differences in the two descriptions above?
- If so, why do they think that is happening?

Activity:

Students will select words or phrases from the list in the workbook that represent success to them. Have them think about other definitions of success that they might use, and share with the group.

At the bottom of the page, have the students write out a short paragraph on what success means to them, incorporating some of the vocabulary they have identified.

Throughout the high school freshman course and the follow-up modules in the 10th, 11th and 12th grades, students will continually revisit their definition of success. Advise your students that success is a personal measurement. What success means to one person is not what it means to another.

An individual's personal definition of success is not a static belief. As they learn more about themselves, the world around them and the opportunities available to them, their definition of success will change and grow. . . . throughout their lives.

Activity:

Have your students turn back to Jordan Powell's 10-year Plan Summary on pages 24 to 27.

- How did Jordan define success?
- Given Jordan's chosen path, does his plan match his definition of success?
- How likely is Jordan to experience success given his plan?

Class Discussion:

Why is being successful on one's own terms important in an individual's career?

VISION + ENERGY = SUCCESS

Learning Objective:

Students will learn a simple formula to guide them as they develop their own career and life plan.

"VISION + ENERGY = SUCCESS"

Presentation Suggestions:

Ask the students if they have heard the expression "mission, vision, values." Write each word on the board. What do these 3 things mean for organizations? Share some examples from company or organization websites.

Activity:

Brainstorm with the students: What do we mean by vision in this example? What do we mean by the term energy, in this context?

At this point these may be foreign concepts, particularly used from this perspective. Ask: "Do YOU have a vision for your own future?"

This is the one of the key mottos of the freshman course. Don't worry if some can't grasp this. They will go into more depth in high school.

For a copy of a Vision + Energy = Success Poster for your classroom, contact Academic Innovations at (800) 967-8016.

Your Successful Future

Learning Objective:

Students will imagine what a regular day in their lives will look like when they are 29 years old. They will begin the process of developing a quantitative vision for their futures.

Presentation Suggestions:

Before you start the envisioning process with your students, it will be helpful to have them think about themselves at age 29. That's more than double their current age, so this will feel old and a long way in the future.

Ask them:

- How many years it will be after they graduated high school before they turn 29?
- How many years will they have spent in higher education or training after high school by age 29?
- At age 29, how many years they might have been working full-time in their chosen career?

Activity:

Now ask each student to sit quietly and shut their eyes in order to think about their future. What do they see themselves doing at age 29?

Once they've done this for two to three minutes, ask your students to quick-write a paragraph explaining what a day in their life at age 29 looks like. An easy prompt in the workbook asks them to think about the morning, afternoon, and evening at this age. What are they doing at that time during a typical day?

Once the assignment is complete (about 10 to 15 minutes), ask for volunteers to read their paragraph.

As you begin, be careful not to step on anyone's dreams. A goal may seem unrealistic for a particular student, but many, many people who demonstrate little potential (even in college) go on to excel in their future careers. You'll need to remind students from time to time that success requires action (energy) in addition to vision. At some point, it may also be appropriate to encourage some students to aim higher if you sense they lack confidence in their own capabilities, but now is not necessarily the time.

Do not call on everyone, because some students may have written very little and you do not want to expose or embarrass them. Explain that it is not uncommon at this age to have not thought a lot about their future. Let them know that the freshman transition course they'll take when they enter high school will help them think more deeply about their futures.

Brainstorm: Why is it a good idea to start thinking about your future before you enter high school?

Points you'll want either students (ideally) or you to make at the end of the brainstorm:

- Graduation from high school is necessary in order to get a good job. A good job is necessary to become self-sufficient and lead a satisfying life.
- Depending on the kind of career you want, you'll probably have to go to college or get some post-secondary training, so it's good to know that sooner versus later.
- The courses you take and the grades you earn in high school will determine if you qualify to go directly to a 4-year university or not.
- The grades you earn in high school will determine whether you will need to take math and English remediation classes in community college if your goal isto transfer to a 4 year university.
- Courses you take in high school will help you build the skills needed for the career of your choice.

The Role of High School in your Future Vision

Learning Objective:

Students will start to think ahead to some of the possible options available to them in high school

Presentation Suggestions:

It is not too early to start envisioning what kinds of benefits a student gets in high school. Naturally there is the academic learning, and hopefully your middle school students are starting to understand why that is vital to their future success and therefore happiness.

Class Discussion:

- Why is it important to get good grades in high school?
- What does a grade for a class represent?
- In academic classes what skills do you learn? Will those be helpful in the workforce?
- Think about the job interview activity we did earlier. What if the person you were interviewing couldn't read, write or speak well? Would you have hired them?

Skills acquisition is more than what is learned in the classroom. Important skills are learned by joining clubs and volunteering for community organizations.

If you can get a counselor from the high school to come in as a guest speaker for this session to do a presentation, that would be a great opportunity for students to hear about some of the opportunities available to them. Otherwise it would be a good idea to get a list of clubs/activities from the high school so that you can share that with your students to give them some ideas.

Activity:

Have the students brainstorm some different things that they may participate in or that may happen while they are in high school, and write the ideas on the board:

Clubs and organizations
Career academies
Classes in subjects they have not yet taken, such as psychology or sociology
Classes in specialized areas such as dance, sports, orchestra
Internships or part-time work
AP or honors classes
Work on the high school newspaper or yearbook
Help with events on campus
Volunteer in the community (community service hours)
Classes that give them college credit such as articulated or dual enrollment or concurrent enrollment classes
Leadership opportunities such as peer counseling or student government
They may get their driver's license
They may take classes that give them an industry qualification, such as classes in dental assisting, auto etc.
They get to choose what they want to do after high school
They get to choose where they will go after high school

Once they've had a chance to learn of the existence of these opportunities, they are ready to write their own vision for what they want their high school experience to be like.

Common Core State Standards for English

CCSS.ELA-LITERACY.W.8.3 Write narratives to develop real or imagined experiences or events using effective technique, relevant descriptive details, and well-structured event sequences.

Chapter Four
Positive Self-concept

Chapter Learning Objectives:

Students will identify their self-concept as positive or negative and practice reframing negative beliefs.

From Wikipedia

One's self-concept (also called self-construction, self-identity, self-perspective or self-structure) is a collection of beliefs about oneself[1][2] that includes elements such as academic performance,[3][4][5][6][7] gender roles, sexuality,[8][9][10] and racial identity.[11] Generally, self-concept embodies the answer to "Who am I?."[12]

One's self-concept is made up of self-schemas, and one's past, present, and future selves.

Self-concept is distinguishable from self-awareness, which refers to the extent to which self-knowledge is defined, consistent, and currently applicable to one's attitudes and dispositions.[13] Self-concept also differs from self-esteem: self-concept is a cognitive or descriptive component of one's self (e.g. "I am a fast runner"), while self-esteem is evaluative and opinionated (e.g. "I feel good about being a fast runner").

Self-concept is made up of one's self-schemas, and interacts with self-esteem, self-knowledge, and the social self to form the self as whole. It includes the past, present, and future selves, where future selves (or possible selves) represent individuals' ideas of what they might become, what they would like to become, or what they are afraid of becoming. Possible selves may function as incentives for certain behavior.[12][14]

The perception people have about their past or future selves is related to the perception of their current selves. The temporal self-appraisal theory[15] argues that people have a tendency to maintain a positive self-evaluation by distancing themselves from their negative self and paying more attention to their positive one. In addition, people have a tendency to perceive the past self less favorably[16] (e.g. "I'm better than I used to be") and the future self more positively[17] (e.g. "I will be better than I am now").

Positive Self-talk

Learning Objective:

Students will assess whether their feelings about themselves are positive or negative

Presentation Suggestions:

To begin this chapter, it would be helpful for the class to discuss what self-concept means.

Write the following dictionary definition on the board: "an idea of the self, constructed from the beliefs one holds about oneself and the responses of others." In other words: our beliefs (not necessarily the truth) about ourselves based on our own (possibly faulty) beliefs, and the responses of others (also possibly very inaccurate).

Ask the class if they can think of some examples of this for themselves, such as name calling – they do <u>not</u> share these out loud. Then ask them to think of something about themselves that might not come to mind when other people think of them. These can be shared! For example – sensitive, open-minded, patient, truthful, imaginative, persuasive, clear-headed, caring, practical, logical etc.

This section contains some quite sophisticated concepts, and students may not have thought about these ideas before. There are two parts to this topic – understanding that we are giving ourselves positive/negative messages, and thinking about how we feel in transactions with others.

Activity:

Have the students close their eyes and listen to what is known as "the little voice in their head" when you give them the following scenario: imagine that they have a test in a week's time in a subject that is challenging for them, that they have to pass with an "A" grade. Then on paper have them write down - what is the voice saying? Is it positive or negative? Whose is the voice in their head? If negative, do they believe the voice, or can they counter it with something positive? Can they control it?

A little later in this chapter, they will do an activity on how to turn negative thoughts into positive ones. For now, just having them learn to listen to that voice in their head and realize whether it is positive or negative is the goal.

The phrase "I'm ok, you're ok" is one of four "life positions" that each of us may take. The four positions are:

I'm not ok, you're ok

I'm not ok, you're not ok

I'm ok, you're not ok

I'm ok, you're ok

For too many young teens the most common position is "I'm not ok, you're ok," which is worth acknowledging with the students. However this is clearly not the most positive way to live our lives, we want to be in the "I'm ok, you're ok" square. The students need to understand that the life position we occupy affects our communications (transactions) and relationships, and therefore our lives as a whole.

Class Discussion:

How can we be more accepting of ourselves? If the students do not come up with the idea on their own, tell them that this chapter is all about how we can change our mindset about ourselves from negative to positive.

Positive Affirmations

Learning Objective:

Students will be introduced to the concept of positive affirmations and see how they can be used to see life in a more positive light.

Note: They will learn how to write positive affirmations in their freshman course.

Presentation Suggestions:

This activity is in three steps.

Step 1: students rate how positive they feel about life

Optional in between steps activity: a short YouTube video can be shown in between the first time that the students rate themselves, and before they develop their list of 10 things they like about their own life: "Jessica's Daily Affirmation"

https://www.youtube.com/watch?v=qR3rK0kZFkg

Step 2: students list 10 things they like about their own life

Step 3: students then rate again how positive they feel about life. Then they answer whether the number went up and if so, why.

The expected/hoped for outcome is that the students will rate their feelings about their lives more positively when they have had a chance to "count their blessings."

Class Discussion:

Did their numbers go up? Why is that? What does that mean for their daily outlook on life?

Write the phrase "count your blessings" on the board and ask how many of them do that regularly? Would that be beneficial? The practice of gratitude, appreciating what they have, is a positive strategy. Many high functioning individuals do this every day.

Turning Negative Thoughts into Positive Ones

Learning Objective:

Students will learn how reframe negative thoughts into positive ones.

Presentation Suggestions:

The students have already practiced "listening in" on that voice in their heads, be it positive or negative. Now they need to learn how to change it into a positive voice if it is negative.

It would be helpful for you to model: share with them a negative thought you have about yourself, and model how you turn it around.

For example: "I am not a good cook" changes to "Cooking is a skill I will practice more so not only will I (or my family) enjoy meals more but I will feel comfortable inviting friends over for a meal."

Also, you could model how you helped a friend to see something in a different light – or how someone helped you to see something differently. Often it is easier to do this with other people than to do it for ourselves.

Activity:

Carefully review the steps with your students and provide an additional example for how you turn a negative thought around.

Step 1 – have them think of a negative belief they have about themselves

Step 2 – have them say out loud "this is a negative thought, not a fact"

Step 3 – replace the negative thought with a positive action they can take

Ask one student (outgoing and not easily embarrassed) to share a negative thought about themselves and then as a class have your students make suggestions of how to replace the thought with a positive one. Brainstorm using examples from a couple of students if you feel that is necessary.

This may be hard for some of them to do. So have them think about a time when they helped someone else see things positively instead of negatively – it could be a friend or family member. If they were able to do it for someone else, they can do it for themselves too.

At the bottom of the page, have them write about the time they helped someone else see something more positively.

Have them discuss and then share in pairs how they turned around a negative thought for someone else. This will increase their self-efficacy, and make them more confident that they can do the same thing for themselves.

Practicing Being Positive

Learning Objective:

Students will practice reframing negative statements and making them positive.

Presentation Suggestions:

Students can attempt to do this individually, but it may be easier for students to do this activity in small groups of three or four, especially if some students regularly have a more positive outlook than others.

However at the bottom of the grid when the students have to come up with a negative thought they have about themselves and reframe it, it would be appropriate to keep it private, unless they want to share or want to get help from the other students on how to turn the negative thought around and make it positive.

Activity:

After the students have completed the grid in their small groups, share their ideas with the class.

Class Discussion:

Was that easy for them to do? If it was difficult, do they have someone in their lives who could help them start to reframe their thoughts into positive ones? Who is the most positive person they know? Get help from them. They'll usually find that this person possesses a lot of what others call wisdom.

Gaining Wisdom from Failures

Learning Objective:

Students will learn that failures are not totally negative experiences. They will reflect on previous failures and the wisdoms that they learned from them.

Presentation Suggestions:

As human beings, we are very good at beating ourselves up over things that we have done wrong or failed at in the past. We carry this weight around with us, and it informs our decision-making and influences all of our possible future activities. We are less likely to attempt something again that we did not succeed in initially, or to try something that is similar to something we tried and failed at before. Can you imagine how liberating it would be to let go of all of that negativity?

Before you do this activity with your students, please do it yourself. You will be surprised how much negative baggage you carry around with you, and how good it feels to acknowledge it and let go of it. You will also be able to share some of your wisdoms with the students to explain the activity to them.

Before the students begin this activity, model for them the wisdoms you gained from one of the failures you identified for yourself. DO NOT SHARE THE FAILURE! It is very important for them to understand that no-one needs to know or will know what their failures were either, just their wisdoms. And for any "failure sheets" that are thrown in the trash, be very careful to remove them at the end of class and dispose of them securely.

Activity:

Students will need a blank sheet of paper. There should be a trash can placed in the middle of the room that they can all access.

Follow the steps in the workbook.

Ask the group which of the 4 choices they made for whether to keep or throw away their failures and wisdoms. Why did they decide to do that? Reinforce that any of the 4 choices are valid.

Class Discussion:

Can they think of anyone famous who failed and learned from their mistakes and then went on to succeed? (You may want to have some names of famous people and their stories ready to share in case the students can't come up with anyone.)

The Positive Side of Failure

Learning Objective:

Students will explore their beliefs about failure by reading quotes about the different aspects of failure and assessing the level to which they agree with them.

Presentation Suggestions:

Some of these quotes contain complex concepts, so it's probably a good idea to have the students take turns in reading them aloud and then discuss their meanings individually as a class before they individually rate each statement as to how much they agree or disagree with it.

Activity:

After students have filled out the grid, have them write their own definition of failure.

Discuss—

- Do they believe that failure is permanent?
- Do they believe that failure leads to learning?
- Do they feel ok to fail?

If in the future, every time the fail at something, or something doesn't go as planned, they'll want to get in the habit of immediately asking themselves, "What did I learn from this experience? What will I do differently next time?"

Turning Your Behaviors in a Positive Direction

Learning Objective:

Students will practice coming up with suggestions for positive behavioral change when they have a negative thought.

Presentation Suggestions:

"Behaving as if" is another somewhat complex concept. You can explain to students that this idea is to do with training their brains to grow in a positive direction. Remind them of the idea of neuroplasticity and the boxing video. The trainers at the boxing studio are helping to retrain the brains of the people who have Parkinson's disease. We can do that for ourselves.

If you have a personal example of a time when you were able to do this, it would be helpful to share. Otherwise a possible example could be a person who is shy, who decides to say hello to 6 people a day that they don't know until it becomes a habit. It helps to reduce their shyness over time.

Activity:

This activity may be easier for students to do with a partner or in a small group situation. Encourage them to generate several activities for each topic area, not just one.

When the class reports out, the new, positive activities can be written on the board for everyone to see.

Finally suggest students try this. SMILE!

It has been discovered that when you are smiling it is difficult to think negatively. It all comes down to the fact that smiling can change your brain. When you smile your brain is aware of the activity and keeps track of it. The more you smile, the more effective you are at breaking any tendency you may have to think negatively. If you smile often enough, even if it is fake, you end up rewiring your brain to make positive patterns more often than negative ones.

Chapter Five
Love What You Do and You'll Never Work a Day in Your Life

Chapter Learning Objective:

To introduce the concept of conscious career selection based on an individual's passions, values and personality.

While this statement may be trite for adults who have made their career choice and retraining or changing our trajectory would be difficult at best, for young teens where the world is still their oyster, an understanding of this powerful statement is timely. They are at a place in their life, where with research, reflection and a lot of hard work, they can find the work they can be passionate about and then get the education and training necessary to be competitive in the workforce for a position.

One of your key roles as an instructor of this course is to keep your antenna up to discover the clues for each student that will help them start identifying their passions. Find those ah ha moments and point them out to students. It just might be a trigger to identifying work that they would find fulfilling.

Love What You Do and You'll Never Work a Day in Your Life

Learning Objective:

Students will reflect on what it means to have a job that you love.

Presentation Suggestions:

As the students in the middle school, they are in an enviable place as they have the years ahead in high school to prepare themselves for a life that matches who they are and what drives them. They may not have role models of parents or family members who love their work, or who are even employed, so it is important to discuss the concept that work can be fulfilling and rewarding.

Activity:

Write this axiom on the board:

Love what you do and you'll never work a day in your life.

Question: *Is it important to love what you do for a living? Why?*

As a class, discuss these topics in this order:

1. What do you think the author meant by this statement?
2. Who, among the adults you know, loves their job? (If they don't know someone in their life for whom this is true, encourage them to think about individuals in the news, or a celebrity).
3. Think about that person for a moment: How does their love of their job reflect in other parts of their lives?

These are sophisticated concepts, so don't assume that all your students will be able to get involved in the conversation at this point. Be patient and take the time necessary to really allow the discussion to evolve.

Once you've completed the conversation, ask your students to write their thoughts and understanding to the question in the workbook.

Finding Your Passion

Learning Objective:

Students will express why it is important for them personally to have a job that they love.

Presentation Suggestions:

Show Steve Jobs' Stanford Commencement Speech, 2005

Found on YouTube at http://www.youtube .com/watch?v=UF8uR6Z6KLc

In this world-renowned 15-minute video, Steve Jobs tells three stories about finding your passion. You might want to show only the first two stories; there is a natural break at the end of the second story, but each one reinforces the notion to follow your passions.

After viewing and discussing the Jobs video, the students will write about what struck them most in the speech and why.

Activity:

From all they've learned so far, they are ready to write a short essay entitled: *Love What You Do and You'll Never Work a Day in Your Life: Three reasons to find work you love.*

If they are better at keyboarding than handwriting, have them print and paste in their workbook, their final product.

Career Research: Your Most Important Research Project

Learning Objectives:

Students will learn a little more about the Department of Labor's Career One-Stop website and the type of career research it can help with.

Presentation Suggestions:

As a class, use the deep reading strategy of a different student reading each paragraph in the workbook, pausing after each to reflect on what was read. Once students have a grasp of the content on that page, it is time to start:

Exploring the Department of Labor's Career One-Stop website.

Ideally students will spend time themselves on the website to explore labor market information for jobs that they are interested in, and they will watch career videos. However if there is no internet access in the classroom, you will need to demonstrate the website to them.

Activity:

- Go to www.careerinfonet.org
- Click on the top tab "Explore careers"
- Then under "Learn about careers" click on "career profiles" then "occupation profile."
- Choose a couple of different careers to research that might be of interest to the students, such as "film and video editors" or "athletic trainers" or "environmental engineering technicians." It will show occupational information for your state.
- Show them the average salaries in your state, how fast the jobs are growing etc. If they don't know very much about a job, they can read about the tasks and activities. Also show them where it explains the level of education or training needed. It may surprise them to see how many well-paying jobs do not require a 4-year degree.

Optional Activity:

Students compare two jobs that they are interested in. They complete a side-by-side grid with the following headings:

Job title		
Salary		
Growth rate		
Training/education required		
Types of tasks the job requires		
Why I like this job		

Job Shadowing Online

Learning Objective:

Students will learn a little more about the Department of Labor's Career One-Stop website and the type of career research it can help with, particularly their excellent job title specific videos.

Presentation Suggestions:

As they say, "Seeing is believing," and job shadowing is an excellent way for students to get an idea of what a specific career entails and to determine is that a match for them.

One of the best ways to get a sense if a career is right for you is to put yourself in that environment and watch how others do this job. This is known as job shadowing. But this can be difficult arrange because of the time required to find an opportunity or the availability of a specific career near you.

As a backup option, watching one of the excellent video about a specific career created by the Department of Labor (over 600) is a great alternative. Having the availability 24/7 allows the learner access to this vital information when the interest is highest.

Activity:

- Show a short video from the Department of Labor (DOL) about one of the careers that your students identified (when they discussed the career of someone who loves their work).
- You can find these videos by going to the Career One Stop web site at: http://www.careeronestop.org/Videos/CareerandClusterVideos/career-and-cluster-videos.aspx_
- By clicking on the specific *Career Cluster* title of interest, you'll find the videos available to students in a drop-down menu.
- Show the DOL video about the high school teaching profession, explaining why you love teaching. Find it under "Education and Training (cluster video)."
- You can also find these videos under the **Occupational Profile** for a specific career that has a video. Look for the **Career Video** link, found near the top of each profile. The drawback of this is that not all career titles have a video. For instance if you query *teachers*, the data that comes up is for *teachers* in general, with no video. The video above is found under "Secondary School Teacher."

Career Exploration is a Long-term Project

Learning Objective:

Students will learn that career exploration is not a one-time event and they'll refine their career choices and their plans throughout high school.

Presentation Suggestions:

After reading the text on page 81 assign a written critique answering the question: *Is it important to love what you do for a living? Why?*

Consider having a couple students read their work to the class. Look for opportunities to have students who don't usually get chosen to read. This type of writing assignment may bring out the best in less motivated students.

Your students are still at the beginning of the career exploration, life-planning process. They have a lot to learn about this decision-making process; it is the ultimate research project. So, remind students that they are going to learn how to research and choose the career path that will match their goals, personalities and lifestyle expectations in their *Get Focused…Stay Focused!* ™ coursework in high school.

Common Core State Standards for English

CCSS.ELA-LITERACY.W.8.7 Conduct short research projects to answer a question (including a self-generated question), drawing on several sources and generating additional related, focused questions that allow for multiple avenues of exploration.

Chapter Six
Cultivate a Positive Attitude Towards Learning

Chapter Learning Objectives:

Students will identify their intrinsic and extrinsic motivators. They will explore their long-term motivators and their attitude towards learning. They will practice setting a short-term goal for themselves including how they will keep themselves motivated to achieve it.

Staying motivated to accomplish a goal is key to success. And when you think about it, staying motivated to complete high school with the skills required to be successful in post-secondary education and on into the workforce is the ultimate challenge for an individual. This requires a positive attitude towards learning and for far too many students this is missing. Students need to buy-into the notion that an education is important and valued.

Advertisers know the answer to the question: how do you get someone to buy into a product, service or movement. They answer the question: *What's in it for me?* Why should I expend the resources or energy to acquire this item? (In the case of education, knowledge and skills.)

In this chapter and the ones that follow, you'll start the process of answering the question: A good education? What's in it for me? Using a student's goals and dreams for their future, you and your students will explore questions that normally even college students don't address.

Just as you can lead a horse to water but you can't make them drink...you can sit a student in the classroom but you can't make him or her think? They have to want to learn. They need to understand what learning means to their lives. They have to understand the consequences of not getting a good education.

The strategies learned in this course and the work they do on their 10-year plan in high school will provide the context to help build the motivation required to stay the course. Not only will they value education, but they will have the blueprint/plan and therefore the expectation of success.

Maintaining Your Motivation Over Time

Learning Objective:

Students will reflect on the motivators they used in the past over the long term.

Presentation Suggestions:

To begin this topic, refer back to the Angela Lee Duckworth video on Grit – remind students of her quote: "Live life like a marathon, not a sprint." In this chapter students will be exploring techniques to maintain motivation over the long term.

Share situations that required you to stay motivated over a period of time. For instance, you wanted to drop some weight or to learn an instrument or some other skill. What strategies did you use to keep motivated? What were some of the things you told yourself to keep yourself positive and motivated?

Now bring it back to education, because that is a long term project that required individuals to stay motivated and focused on a goal. Share with the students how you kept motivated during your Bachelor's degree and your teaching credential.

Make Notes Here:

Explain to your students that they have already had practice in staying motivated over the long-term, but that it may not be something that they thought about consciously. In this chapter they will think more explicitly about their motivators so that they can use them when needed.

Activity:

When students thought about challenges and perseverance, they had to come up with something that was difficult for them but which they were able to achieve with effort and persistence.

Have them think back to that challenge on page 36 and answer the prompts on this activity. Once students have completed their work as a class ask students to share their examples of:

- When they wanted to give up, what kept them going?
- What did they tell themselves to keep motivated? (The positive little voice in their heads!)
- How did they cope with staying motivated towards a goal that was a long way ahead?

A Positive or Negative Outlook?

Learning Objective:

Students learn how their attitudes affect their motivation.

Presentation suggestion:

Assign one student the role of Optimist and another student the role of Pessimist. Read the first paragraph yourself and after each student who is reading their part, ask the class as a group to rate how motivated each person sounds.

Which of the two students would most likely to be successful and pass their math class?

Remind students that math is a class that starts to sort students. Depending on the level of math taken in high school, students may limit their post-secondary options.

Read the following passage aloud to the students:

Attitude

A recent three-year study* was conducted of 5,247 hiring managers from 312 public, private, business and healthcare organizations who hired more than 20,000 employees during the study period.

The study found that 46% of new hires failed within 18 months. Even more surprising than the failure rate, was that when new hires failed, 89% of the time it was for attitudinal reasons and only 11% of the time for a lack of skill. Of those who failed, 26% failed because they couldn't accept feedback, 23% because they were unable to understand and manage emotions, 17% because they lacked the necessary motivation to excel, 15% because they had the wrong temperament for the job, and only 11% because they lacked the necessary technical skills.

Attitude, not skills, therefore, is the top predictor of a new hire's success or failure. Known as Soft skills (which the authors argue is a bad term for these necessary skills) they are the capabilities that attitude can enhance or undermine.

As Herb Kelleher, former Southwest Airlines CEO used to say, "We can change skill levels through training, but we can't change attitude."

**The study was conducted by Leadership IQ, a global leadership training and research company.*

Activity:

Use a demonstration of "The glass half full" for this exercise. Without saying anything else, fill a tall glass half way up with water, and then ask: *Describe this glass and the water in it.*

Have your students write their answer in the workbook. They will write something along the lines of they see it as either half-full or half-empty.

Then show the YouTube video called The Science of Happiness: Is Your Glass Half-Full or Half-Empty?

Link: https://www.youtube.com/watch?v=V9xhpLpZZSg

Class Discussion:

What did students think about the results of the experiment?

Motivators

Learning Objective:

Students will identify which motivators work well for them, in varying degrees, and which have no effect.

Presentation suggestion:

We are all motivated by different things. It is important for students to be able to know what motivates them when they are facing challenges. They may be motivated by different things at different times in their lives, and some things that motivate other people may not motivate them at all!

Activity:

Individually have your students check the boxes next to each potential motivator, evaluating to what extent each motivator affects them.

Now have them review their checkmarks in the first column—*Works really well for me.* Do these have anything in common with each other? Can you identify a simpler pattern? For those students who find a similarity, ask them to share their finding with the other members of the class.

Class Discussion:

Are there other things not on the list that motivates you? What are some of those motivators?

Strategies for Staying Motivated

Learning Objective:

Students will learn the difference between extrinsic and intrinsic motivators and identify which work best for them in certain scenarios.

Presentation Suggestions:

One of the main ideas it will be important for students to understand from this section is that extrinsic motivators tend to be short-term, whereas intrinsic motivators tend to be long-term.

First you'll want to review what intrinsic and extrinsic means

> Intrinsic motivation is the self-desire to seek out new things and new challenges, to analyze one's capacity, to observe and to gain knowledge. It is driven by an interest or enjoyment in the task itself, and exists within the individual rather than relying on external pressures or a desire for reward or praise.
>
> Extrinsic motivation refers to the performance of an activity in order to attain a desired outcome. It is the opposite of intrinsic motivation. Extrinsic motivation comes from influences outside of the individual. Common extrinsic motivations are rewards (for example money). Competition is an extrinsic motivator because it encourages the performer to win and to beat others, not simply to enjoy the intrinsic rewards of the activity. A cheering crowd and the desire to win a trophy are also extrinsic rewards.
>
> Grades are an extrinsic reward driven by extrinsic motivation while the good feeling one gets from mastering a topic is an example of intrinsic reward driven by intrinsic motivation.

Have the students look back at the activity they just did on "Motivators." Have them write 'E" or "I" next to each activity that they rated as working, or working really well for them. You will probably have to help them analyze which motivators fall into which category, "E" or "I."

Class Discussion:

- Do they have more "E" (extrinsic) or "I" (intrinsic) motivators that work for them, or do they have a mix?

Activity: After the students have completed the scenarios, have them discuss with a partner which motivators they would use short-term (the first scenario) versus long-term (the second scenario). Write them under each scenario in the workbook.

Class Discussion:

- Did they think they would use different motivators in each scenario?
- If there was a difference, why do they think that was the case?

While it has been argued that intrinsic motivation produces more long term results, whichever type of motivator works for the students is good. But it is important for them to know what motivates them. Reassure your students that there are no "good" or "bad" motivators. But stress that motivators alone will not get them through challenging tasks. They also need grit!

Motivational Triggers

Learning Objective:

Students learn about motivational triggers and their power to inspire.

Presentation Suggestions:

In this activity students will select from the quotes provided or craft a favorite motivational quote they can use in the future for a trigger and they'll make a motivational poster.

As a class read through the quotes provided, followed by a discussion of each one and what the author meant when they wrote or spoke that bit of wisdom. Have students look up any individuals they don't know, remembering what was said was probably said in the context of the person's profession or the times.

Share with your students your favorite inspiration quotes. What do you say to yourself when you need some inspiration? Write them here:

If you have any motivational posters you have up on the walls of your classroom, this would be a good discussion for this topic:

Class Discussion:

- Are any of them actually motivational for your students?
- If not, can they find one on the Internet that they could share with the class?

Activity:

Showing a motivational video might also be a good activity for the class. There may be one you already know of and like, or you can search YouTube. There are lots to choose from! Some of the best are the graduation speeches at colleges and universities by recognized and accomplished individuals. In the search box write "college graduation speech."

Or you could ask students about a movie or show they have seen that they think was very motivational. Have them share why that worked for them.

Sometimes it is hard for students to do this kind of activity with themselves in mind, so as an alternative, they could choose a saying and make a poster for a friend/family member who needs to stay motivated.

The finished posters can be posted around the class for a week or so before the students put them inside their lockers or on a mirror or wall at home.

Motivational Goal-setting for the Short Term

Learning Objective:

Students will set a short-term goal for themselves and identify how they will keep motivated to achieve it.

Presentation Suggestions:

Ask students to stop, close their eyes and think about something they want to accomplish or an area they want to improve on. Something they want to experience more success in. Direct them to write it down in the workbook under "What is an area I want to improve in?"

This would be a goal for them. Thinking about what they have learned so far, have them answer the four questions in writing.

Once they have completed their written work in their workbook, this may be a good opportunity to talk about **SMART** goals:

Specific—A general goal would be, "Eat healthy." But a specific goal (also known as an objective) would say, "Instead of always snacking on chips and candy, I will eat fruit or nuts instead at least 4 days a week."

Measurable—Establish progress measurement criteria. When you measure your progress, you stay on track, reach your target dates, and experience the exhilaration of achievement that spurs you on to continued effort required to reach your goal. "I will eat fruit and nuts one day a week, then two days, then three days until by week four I am eating them four times a week."

Attainable—You can attain most any goal you set when you plan your steps wisely and establish a time frame that allows you to carry out those steps.

Realistic—To be realistic, a goal must represent an objective toward which you are both willing and able to work.

Timely—A goal should be grounded within a time frame.

It is important to share your goals – when we talk about our goals with other people, we start training our brains to move in the direction of that goal.

> One of the authors taught a college class once and had all of the students write career action plans with next steps, and share with each other. One student came up to her several years later and shared that he had lost his action plan almost immediately, but that he found it again a few weeks previously, and he had achieved everything on the list, because he had set goals and shared them.

Even better is having someone to hold us accountable for our goals. Do the students have anyone who can hold them accountable for reaching their goals? A family member, or friend? You?

Activity:

Given the goal they chose for themselves for this activity and their prompts, have them share their goal with a partner. Then have them assess each other's goal to see if it is a SMART goal. If not, have them add in more parameters to make it a SMART goal.

Staying Motivated for a Long-term Cherished Goal

Learning Objective:

The understanding of what is needed to stay motivated over the long term.

Presentation Suggestions:

Two things are required, in order to stay motivated long enough to accomplish important long term goals.

1. The goal must be valued... something desired
2. There must be an expectation of success

Think about the last time you tackled a goal that required sustainability over a long period of time. Let's take getting fit or losing weight as an example. Think about it. If you failed at your goal it was probably because one of the two conditions above was not present. And it is most likely the expectation of success.

Today when entering high school freshman or surveyed most say they plan to go to college. They know the value of college and why it is necessary.

But for far too many students, when it comes to sustaining the effort necessary to complete their education (secondary and post-secondary) in order to qualify for the career of their choice, without a detailed plan that provides a vision and expectation of success, it is likely they will not follow through. Keep in mind only 19% of your students will complete college within 6 years of high school graduation.

The 10-year planning process learned in high school, which is very detailed and in depth, provides a platform that gives students an expectation of success. They learn they, not anyone else, (parent, counselor, teacher) is in control of their future. They have a path to follow that makes sense and is doable.

Activity:

Using the deeper reading strategy, as a class read aloud and discuss the contents of this activity.

Class Discussion:

The decision-making process they will learn: Who am I, what do I want, and how do I get it, can be used when making most of life's decisions. As a class, brainstorm what those are.

> Examples: Where to live. When and if to get married. When and if to have children. Where to work. When to leave a job and move on to another.

Chapter Seven

Identifying Your Passions:

It's the First Step to Finding Work That You Love

Chapter Learning Objective:

To help students learn to identify and articulate those things that are extremely important to them. They will go on to define the concept of "passion" as it relates to an individual's work or career.

When an individual is passionate about the work they do, as learned earlier 'they never work a day in their lives'. But how does one go about identifying their passions, so they can use that knowledge to help them in their career search? This chapter starts that process.

Your students will go even deeper into this concept throughout high school. Remind them that they will discover passions throughout their lives. What is important is that they start becoming aware of what they are.

Optional Long-term Project #1

Using Students' Passions to Create Self-directed Learners

At this point in the course, if you are choosing to do the Optional Project beginning on page 4/117 of this manual, you may want to start that process now because it will take time for your students to research their book, read it and report out. That process can be integrated throughout the rest of the course.

If you school has chosen to divide this curriculum in half, with the first six chapters being taught in the seventh grade and the next six, starting here in the eighth grade, this is an ideal time as well to consider adding this project into your course work.

Identify Your Passions

Learning Objective:

Students will define what is meant by the term "passion" in a career context.

Presentation Suggestions:

Write the two definitions of passion on the board.

- The dictionary defines passion as a *"powerful emotion; boundless enthusiasm; deep overwhelming feeling; or avid interest."*
- *"Passion is the energy and enthusiasm wedded to a sense of purpose that gives life meaning and pleasure."* — Carl Goldberg, clinical psychologist and author

We thought about substituting another word for *passion* but, after lengthy debate, decided it was the most appropriate term. You may get some snickering from a few students because their reference will be in relation to "romance." Be prepared. Use the situation to demonstrate how the things that matter most to an individual can elicit feelings of excitement similar to those usually associated with romantic passion.

If someone alludes to the romantic overtones in the term, ask him or her to describe the feeling. List these on the board and then use them to help the class identify other passions. "What else makes you grin? What other situations make your heart race? What else do you do that makes you lose track of time?"

Activity:

Have students brainstorm and write their own definitions of what a "passion" is, and then share them with the class. This could be done individually or in small groups of two or three. They will also suggest some key words that can be written on the board.

What are You Passionate About?

Learning Objective:

Students will begin the process of identifying their passions.

Presentation Suggestions:

Quick-write Activity: Start identifying passions

Make sure students have a pen and paper in front of them before starting.

With every student ready to write, read these five prompts and ask the students to complete them. (Allow 2 or 3 minutes for students to reflect before responding to each.)

1. My heart pounds with excitement when…
2. I feel especially good about myself when…
3. I get a lump in my throat or feel overcome with emotion when…
4. I lose track of time whenever I am…
5. When I dream about my future, I see myself…

Once students complete the above statements, ask each person to review their statements and start making a list of their passions. They are starting to identify the things and activities that they have boundless energy and enthusiasm for. This list will be vital for not only the lessons that follow, but also their education and career choices later in high school.

If they are having trouble creating the list of their passions, pair them up (stronger students with struggling students). Ask the teams to read each other's responses to the prompts, and then brainstorm the list of passions for their team member.

Their passions can be shared with the class, and you could write the things they are passionate about on the board so that students can see the variety and similarity within their group.

Articulating Your Passions

Learning Objective:

Students will list their passions so they can be used as they make career and life choices.

Presentation Suggestions:

The previous activity got the students thinking about their passions in terms of their emotions. They will reflect on their answers in this activity. However it may be helpful to give them some other prompts to get them thinking.

On the board, write these prompts:

- Things you like to create
- Things you like to fix
- Things you like to invent
- Things you want in your life every day
- Things you like to do by yourself
- Things you like to do with friends
- Things you like to do with your family
- Things you like to do in your community
- Classes you really enjoy
- Clubs or groups you belong to
- Things you want to try out in the future that you haven't had a chance to do yet

Activity:

Students will review the statements they made in the previous activity, "What are you passionate about?" and start making a list of their passions. They are starting to identify the things and activities that they have *boundless energy and enthusiasm for.* This list will be vital for not only the lessons that follow, but also their education and career choices later in high school.

You'll want students to turn these lists into you so you can review and also make recommendations as to passion topics. Plus, knowing what each student is passionate about can help you personalize your work with them.

> *Note: They'll complete a similar activity in their **Career Choices** course in the 9th grade (see Chapter 2 of **Career Choices**). Keep in mind that we can't ask ourselves these questions too often. Each time students complete this activity, they'll probably discover something new about themselves and their goals. They'll want to review and refine what motivates them and what drives them throughout their lives.*

Do the Math

Learning Objective:

Students will calculate how many hours they project that they will work in their lifetimes, and compare that with how many hours they will spend on career planning in high school.

Presentation Suggestions:

The years spent working are many. The hours are long. For most it will consume a major portion of their adult life. Spending the time to both identify a career and prepare oneself for a career that they could be passionate about is time well spent.

The math problem in this activity will graphically demonstrate how much time will be spent on planning and researching their career versus how much time actually working.

If they have friends in other school districts that are not doing a 10-year Plan, they or their parents may question, why they are spending so much time on this process. When shown in context of their whole work life, it is easy to justify the time and resources.

Note:

This topic is going to touch on some concepts that students may not have considered yet, that need to be discussed before the activity, such as:

- At what age will they finish post-secondary college or training?
- Will they work full-time, part-time or not at all during that time period?
- At what age will they retire? (They may not know average retirement ages.)
- Will they take time out of the workforce to raise children?
- Are they any other reasons they will take time out of the workforce? (For example, year abroad)
- Do they plan to work part-time or full-time?
- Will they have a job where they get breaks in employment? (Teaching, counseling)

Activity:

Students will factor in the variables mentioned, and come up with an estimate of the total number of hours they will work in their lifetimes. Then they will figure out the total number of hours they will spend career planning as a percentage of that total.

They will not be able to come up with a very accurate figure, because they will not yet know information such as how many weeks they will get for vacation, etc., but it will give them a reality check as to how many hours they will be working, and what a proportionately small amount of time they will spend planning for that career.

Your Ideal Day

Learning Objective:

Learning to envision the ideal.

Presentation Suggestions:

One of the best ways to start to develop a plan is to envision the ideal and then adjust from there. If individuals are pushed to imagine the best case scenario, or to shoot for the stars, then the final plan, based more on reality, is more likely to challenge them and get closer to what they really want.

Students write an essay about their ideal day using the list of passions they identified in the previous activity. The essay should describe a day that involves as many of their favorite experiences as possible.

Students may need to hear a couple of examples before they start. You could write your own, so that they could hear some of the things you like to do other than teaching!

Or you give them a couple of outlines such as the ones below, but explain that you need more detail:

> *Nina's day, for example, might include winning a political debate while wearing her red shoes. As she walks home she takes photos of ducks at her local park; before joining her family to watch the Lakers' game on TV.*
>
> Juan's day might include him composing a new song to play on his guitar; working on his website with his best friend; winning a league soccer match that afternoon before going to bed and reading a new mystery story.

A Word about Finding your Passions

Learning Objective:

Understanding that identifying one's passions is a life-long process.

Presentation:

Use the deep reading strategy for the text on this page.

Students may not realize that the things they are excited about now may not be what they love to do in 10 or 20 years' time. So have them think back to something they loved to do when they were in elementary school that they don't do any more. Or something they did last year that now they don't do any more. Or a food that they didn't like, but now they love.

Activity:

Ask students to interview their parent(s) or another adult, to find out if they can articulate their passions. They should ask:

Can you list what you are most passionate about?

If they can't, students might want to share the trigger statements found on page 96 of their workbook to see if that helps

Ask the interviewee if they've identified any new passions in the last year or two? If so, what? How?

Your Plan in Your Pocket

Learning Objective:

Students learn that the 10-year Plan they develop will be available to them as a phone app so that they can revisit it at any time.

Presentation Suggestions:

Share with your students the things you used to like to do as a teenager—and how technology has changed many of our pastimes in ways we could not have imagined. It may be hard for them to imagine the world without cellphones or the Internet, but that world was not so long ago.

You can download a prototype example of the My10yearPlan but it will not be populated, unless you yourself have completed your own 10-year Plan. Which you can do with this offer:

> As a middle school instructor, who has adopted the middle school bridge program, you qualify for your own complimentary copy of the college/adult version of the ***Career Choices*** series, ***Career Choices and Changes***, along with a license to My10yearPlan.com Interactive.
>
> To claim your copy write a one page description of your middle school program and your goals for your students and send by snail mail (so it doesn't get lost ;-) to Middle School Bridget Program Support Team, Academic Innovations, 59 S. 100 E. Saint George Utah. 84770

You'll find the decision-making process, learned in the freshman course, (high school or college) is ageless. It doesn't matter what age you are the process is applicable and valuable. Why not determine what your next phase/career is upon retirement?

Activity:

Have students brainstorm why it would be helpful to have their 10-year Plan available to them as a phone app.

Who would they share their plan with?

Common Core State Standards for English

CCSS.ELA-LITERACY.W.8.10 Write routinely over extended time frames (time for research, reflection, and revision) and shorter time frames (a single sitting or a day or two) for a range of discipline-specific tasks, purposes, and audiences

Chapter Eight
Resiliency and Overcoming Obstacles

Chapter Learning Objective:

Research has identify the trait of resiliency, the ability to bounce back from challenging situations, as a key indicator of success. The question is: How do you cultivate resiliency in adolescents who may not exhibit that trait?

The first step of any behavioral change is for the individual to recognize any shortcomings. In very basic terms that is the goal of this chapter. The activities included in this chapter are just the beginning to helping students develop self-mastery.

Students will explore how resilient they are; they will learn how controlling their emotions can affect them being able to overcome obstacles; and they will practice handling emotions to overcome obstacles. They will also explore what a "hardy personality" means

Resiliency Quiz

Learning Objective:

Students will analyze how resilient they feel they are.

Presentation Suggestions:

Ask the students what they think of when they hear the word "resiliency." What does it mean to them? It may be helpful to write the dictionary definition on the board: "The power or ability to return to the original form, position etc. after being compressed or stretched; ability to recover readily from adversity, depression, illness, or the like; buoyancy."

A phrase they might recognize more easily might be how they "bounce back" after a setback.

Activity:

Show the students the video: "Instructions for a bad day" by Shane Koyczan.

https://www.youtube.com/watch?v=cnFAGgKB-wA

You may also want to look up the poem online and print it out for them to read after watching the video. Ask them what ideas they heard that they can use to make a bad day bearable.

Have them take the resiliency quiz. If it is better, read each statement aloud as students listen and circle those that sound most like them.

Have students score their quiz, using the Rubric on the next page.

Brainstorm: What are some things they can do to be more resilient?

Hang in There!

Learning Objective:

Students will identify their emotions and attitudes around overcoming obstacles.

Presentation Suggestions:

Students have already identified a challenge that they had to overcome. This chapter is about their attitude as a key factor in being able to cope with and overcome challenges, so they will be reflecting upon how they felt emotionally about the amount of effort and time they needed to put into the challenge in order to be successful. It also gets them to think about the emotional rewards of overcoming a challenge.

The idea we want students to grasp here is that they can change their feelings about something, and that they control their emotions about an issue.

Activity:

Introduce this activity with an example of your own to model.

Have the students think about something they hated to do in the past that now they actually don't mind doing, or that they like doing.

Have some students share their examples.

Class Discussion:

- What changed their minds?
- How did their feelings change?
- Did they make a conscious decision to change their attitude?
- How did they feel when their attitude changed from negative to positive?

Now have them do the activity in the workbook. If they can't think of a new challenge, they can turn back to the one they indicated in Chapter 2.

Some Good Advice

Learning Objective:

Students will select or create a saying that inspires them to overcome obstacles and keep going.

Presentation Suggestions:

As student learned earlier that with motivational triggers, sayings, quotes and sage advice can help one get focused and stay focused. They will use the same strategy as one way to help them overcome obstacles

Share a saying that you find inspirational, or if the classroom has computer and Internet access, have the students look up sayings using the key words "quotes" and "challenges" or "obstacles."

The students will also be asked to identify someone that they rely on for support when they are coping with a challenge. It is extremely important for them to have at least one person that they can turn to when things get tough, whether that is a family member, friend, or trusted adult.

Activity:

Students select or create a saying. They could then illustrate it and the posters could be displayed on the classroom walls.

Your Attitude: A Key Factor to Overcoming Obstacles

Learning Objective:

Students will identify whether their emotions and attitude are mainly positive or negative when faced with a challenge.

Presentation Suggestions:

Read the text and then have your students choose adjectives that describe their feelings when faced with a challenge.

First have them circle the words that they feel reflect their feelings.

Then have the students put "P" for a positive feeling or "N" for a negative feeling next to each word they circled.

Do they have more positive or negative emotions?

If they have more negative than positive emotions right now, have them think back to the activity they did earlier in the workbook on turning negative thoughts into positive ones (Chapter 4). Have them use the technique of reframing to think differently and positively about the challenge and their emotions towards it.

Optional Discussion:

After your students have completed their written work on the activity share the following with information with your students. Do any of your students think they use any of the negative thinking types?

We have already talked a little about attitude. But did you know that we each generate between 25,000 to 50,000 thoughts per day? If a large number of these thoughts are negative, we affect our health, happiness and well-being. Multiple studies show that negative thinking can lead to a damaged immune system, and can even shorten our lives!

There are 4 main types of negative thinking:

Filtering—screening out possible positives outcomes in a difficult situation. "This is not going to end well."

Personalizing—blaming yourself every time something bad happens. "This is all my fault."

Catastrophizing—expecting the worst possible outcome in a difficult situation. "I am going to fail this class!"

Polarizing—thinking that anything less than perfection is a failure. "I did terribly."

Positive thinking on the other hand can result in longer life, happier moods, lowered stress, a boosted immune system, a stronger sense of well-being and better coping skills during stressful events. Because of the connection between the body and mind, the psychological benefits of positive thinking tend to reinforce its physical benefits, and vice versa.

What Would You Do?

Learning Objective:

Students will practice putting their emotions aside to focus on taking control of a situation.

Presentation Suggestions:

One of the main points for students to take away from this activity is that no matter what their emotional state, they need to develop the skills to put their feelings aside and brainstorm solutions to a problem.

Activity:

Students read the scenario and score how they would feel in that situation. Then they brainstorm ideas for how to resolve the situation. Encourage them to think of multiple solutions—it is important that they learn that there is not just one way to fix things.

Some of the students may find this difficult, so after they have responded to how the situation would make them feel, putting them into groups to brainstorm will help them see multiple possibilities. Have them report out and write possible ideas on the board.

Having them work together to come up with possible solutions segues nicely into the next activity, "Teamwork and problem solving."

Teamwork and Problem Solving

Learning Objective:

Students will learn how input from others can be helpful in finding solutions.

Presentation Suggestions:

Have the students take a piece of paper and fold it in half lengthways. Have them write "Goal" on the top of the left column. Under the heading, have students write down a goal that they would like to work towards that they are not moving forwards with, that they are comfortable sharing with the group. It could be to learn a new sport or hobby, get a better grade in a particular class, win a competition, etc.

In the right hand column, have them write the heading "Obstacle." Have them identify the obstacle/s that are preventing them from moving forwards, and write those on the sheet also. Ask them to pass their papers forward to you. These are anonymous.

Choose one paper as an example. Write the goal and the obstacle on the board. On a separate sheet of paper, have students brainstorm as many solutions to overcoming the obstacle to reach the goal as they can. Have them pass the papers forward, and write the solutions on the board.

This activity shows students that there are many different ways of thinking about a problem, and that teamwork, or problem solving with other people, can often be more effective than us trying to solve problems on our own.

Activity:

Students ask 3 people whose advice they trust to give them input on possible solutions to a challenge they currently face. (This may have to be assigned as homework, if they want to discuss with family members or trusted adults.)

They alone determine whether the advice they have been given would work for them or not. It is important that they understand that they can discount other people's advice, as only they know what is best for themselves.

The Hardy Personality

Learning Objective:

Students will learn what the term: "hardy personality" means.

Presentation Suggestions:

Using the deep reading strategy, read the text about the Hardy personality.

Class Discussion:

Without sharing names, ask students identify individuals with an *external locus of control.* Perhaps celebrities who are struggling with issues, come to mind.

This is an opportunity to show videos that either you already know of, or you could research one or two appropriate ones, using the search term "resiliency" on YouTube. There are many examples.

Activity:

After the reading, students can identify someone they know (maybe someone famous or someone they know personally) who they think demonstrates having a hardy personality.

Have them share in pairs, and then several students can report out on why they think that person is resilient, and how they demonstrate it.

Developing a Hardy Personality

Learning Objective:

Students will reflect on the 8 traits and skills needed to develop a hardy personality.

Presentation Suggestions:

Students will be reading about the 8 traits and skills needed to develop a hardy personality in this section. In order to understand these concepts better, it will be helpful to ask them questions and have them reflect on times in the past when they have been able to use these 8 skills.

Activity:

Students give examples of when they used some of the traits and skills of a hardy personality.

For example:

1. Learning to recognize and tolerate anxiety and act anyway—what's a situation they have been in where they were anxious or stressed but succeeded? How did they do that? What tools/strategies did they use to minimize the stress?
2. Learning to be discriminating and make choices on what is best for you—when have they had to choose between two options? How did they do their decision-making? Did they look at facts/use their instincts/take other people's opinions?
3. Learning to set boundaries and limits—when did they have to say no to someone? Was it easy for them or hard? If it was hard, how did they do it anyway? What did they tell themselves?

You could also give the students a grid to fill out where they rate themselves from 1-5 on each of the 8 areas, with 5 being that they feel they possess a high level of the trait or skill. Then those who scored highly on certain categories could share their strategies/examples after completing the activity above.

Remind your students that this is just an overview of what they will learn about in their freshman course. They will go into these topics in more detail in high school.

Chapter Nine

Beginning Your Career Search

Chapter Learning Objective:

Students will learn how to use their list of passions to identify potential careers they might find appealing. They will also learn how to identify traits and skills and think about how those apply to careers and to the development of an education plan.

This chapter was meant as an overview of the process, not necessarily to have students go in depth into the process of choosing a career. That will be done in high school. Therefore the questions are basic, using what they know about certain high-profile careers.

When speaking about skills and traits, if you have time you can have students go online to CareerOneStop.org to research the specific careers addressed in this chapter. But you don't have to. To get the gist of what they need to understand about the career research process, you rely on what is commonly known about firefighters, computer programmers, and nurses.

Your Career Search

Learning Objective:

Students will learn how to link their passions with possible career areas.

Presentation Suggestions:

Read the text using the deep reading strategy.

Over the next couple of years students will have the opportunity to explore a variety of occupations as they create your 10-year Plan. After a lot of self-reflection and research they'll identify an "ideal career" in the 9th grade. Bringing in the realities of the work place, in the 10th grade they'll study high demand and higher wage careers. In the 11th grade, they'll focus on the opportunities of STEM careers (Science, Math, Engineering and Technology) before finally settling on a career on which to do you college/post-secondary educational planning. By that time they'll have probably spent well over 120 hours exploring the options available before settling on how they want to spend a good percentage of their time over the coming decades of their 20s, 30s, 40s, 50s, etc.

Does that sound daunting? Tell them not to worry. They are about to start learning a systematic decision-making process that will help all this come together. Between now and the time they graduate from high school they'll have the opportunity, with the help of you, their instructors, counselors and mentors to explore a variety of career options. In the end they'll have the background and skill set to find a career that matches their passions, skills, traits, values, personality, lifestyle expectations and goals.

To begin this search, let's look closer at two of the ingredients that will influence their choice.

1. What careers match your passions?
2. What careers require the skills and traits you have or hope to learn?

Activity:

Ask students to interview their parent(s) or other significant adult that they know, asking these questions:

Looking back when you were in high school, how much thought did you give to your future career?

What was the process you used to determine your first career path?

If they have changed careers, ask: What process did you most recently use to determine your career path?

Brainstorming Careers that Match Your Passions

Learning Objective:

Students will learn how to link their passions with possible career areas.

Presentation Suggestions:

Revisit the quote: *Love what you do and you'll never work a day in your life.* Ask your students to reflect on that quote now that they have identified their passions.

You (or one of your guests noted in the activity that follows) can make a presentation to students on how to choose career options to research, based on the passions they identify.

An important point to include in the discussion:

What are the traits and skills of the activities I'm passionate about that give me pleasure?

There is also vital vocabulary that needs to be explained.

"What is a skill?"

The ability to do something well; expertise; a particular ability such as *the basic skills of cooking.*

"What is a trait?"

A distinguishing quality or characteristic, typically one belonging to a person. Sometimes a trait is a genetically determined characteristic.

Activity:

While you can break your students into small groups to discuss this, because middle school students have little experience with understanding the depth of the thousands of jobs available, consider the following formal activity:

1. Ask each student to choose the top three or four passions that they would like to address in the work they do. Print those three or four activities or topics in large block letters horizontally on a sheet of paper (8½" x 11").
2. Then, one at a time, each student comes to the front of the class, holding their sheet as a sign in front of them.
3. Ask the students in the class along with a panel of adults you've recruited* to quickly brainstorm careers that would include either directly or indirectly the elements of those passions.
4. Recorder: Ask someone to be the recorder, recording the ideas that each student finds intriguing. They don't have to write all the ideas down, just those the student agrees sound interesting. They should provide this list to the teacher at the end of the session.
5. At the same time, ask the students in the class to follow along during each other's brainstorming sessions. As they hear careers or skills named for another student that pique their interest, they should be instructed to write that career down on the reverse of their own passions sign. That way, by the time they get to the front of the class, they can first share what they've heard so far that sounds interesting—which will help those brainstorming to focus their suggestions—and then share their original passions.

* For a panel of adults, here are some ideas of people to invite:

- Counselors at your school
- Head of your Career Center or the Career Center of your local community college
- A parent with human resources background or employment specialties
- The CTE director of your local community college
- Someone with a career counseling background from your Workforce Development Board
- An employment specialist, such as someone who runs a temp agency or someone who is a human resource director for a large company

Starting Your List of Possible Career Choices

Learning Objective:

Students will document careers that might match their passion areas; they will select their top 3 careers, and reflect on why they are a good match for their passions.

Presentation Suggestions:

Students may have heard job titles that are unfamiliar to them, or about which they know very little. When they write down their list of possible job titles, they should star the ones they don't know very much about, and research them on www.careeronestop.org, looking at labor market information or the career videos. They may also have an inaccurate understanding of what the job really entails, and so reading the typical job tasks would be helpful, even if they think they know what the job is all about!

Activity:

After they have completed the activity in their workbook, have your students share with the class their top career choice and explain how it matches their passions.

Using Higher-order Thinking Skills to Get What You Want

Learning Objective:

Students will start learning how to analyze the skills and traits in an activity they are passionate about, and how that can translate to a job that is different than the obvious.

Presentation Suggestions:

Finding the skills and traits included in an activity that students are passionate about is an important consideration, because not all passions can translate to a career.

Use the deep reading strategy to read and discuss the concept presented in the workbook.

The chose a couple of other obvious passion areas that teen gravitate to when identifying careers they want to follow:

Musician
Entertainer
Athlete
Computer gamer
Shopping

For example:

An entertainer or musician is not afraid of performing in front of groups/crowds—they can become a trainer or teacher

Athletes have a competitive spirit: likes to win or come out on top—this can transfer to becoming a salesperson or politician

A computer gamer likes the digital world. This translates to anything in the technological field, from computer coder to systems analyst or mechanical engineer.

Someone who loves to shop could go into retail which is an obvious, but part of the thrill of shopping for many is the "hunt." That brings to mind a passion and skill that could translate to a research scientist or private investigator

Career Research: Matching Skills and Traits

Learning Objective:

Students will learn about that there are 3 types of skills needed in the workforce; Technical, Employability and Transferable.

Presentation Suggestions:

Review the information on this page in class.

For students to grasp the difference between the 3 different types of skills that employers are looking for, use the example of a firefighter:

Technical skills—what does a firefighter have to know how to do?

Employability skills—what kind of characteristics should a firefighter have?

Transferable skills—what can a firefighter do that they could also do in a different career?

Activity:

Write the 3 different types of skill headings on the board and have the students brainstorm ideas for a firefighter for each.

Prior to class you might want to go online to Careeronestop.org and print their lists for firefighters found under that profile and the links to Knowledge Skills and Abilities to help with this brainstorm. But at this point going into this depth on information, out of context could be overwhelming to the average middle school student. Perhaps show them the information on an overhead/whiteboard, but save this process for their freshman year.

Identifying Traits

Learning Objective:

Students will practice analyzing traits required for a particular job.

Presentation Suggestions:

Students in this chapter are beginning to learn about all of the different things that an employer is looking for in job candidates. Although many different types of people can do the same jobs, jobs have specific requirements that need to be met.

For example:

A customer service person should be cheerful and good at solving problems.

A scientist needs to be good at solving problems, but do they need to be cheerful?*

Activity:

Students will identify traits they think an employer might want in a computer programmer. You could read down the list of possible traits after they have made their choices, and write the traits that students chose on the board, tallying them.

Class Discussion:

Which traits were chosen by most students?

Why did they choose these traits?

Repeat the activity for a nurse.

Do they see a difference in traits needed by an employer for each job?

Identifying Skills

Learning Objective:

Students will practice recognizing and analyzing technical skills required for a particular job.

Presentation Suggestions:

If your classroom has internet access, it would be a good idea to show the students the career videos for a nurse and a computer programmer from the Department of Labor website, www.careeronestop.org, before they start the activity. Have them make notes of skills they are hearing about or seeing as they watch the video.

Activity:

Then they can work in small groups to identify the specific technical skills needed for each of these careers. Groups report out and a list of technical skills generated by the groups can be written on the board.

Taking Control of Your Life/Developing a Skills-based Education Plan

Learning Objective:

Students will identify ways to learn technical skills required by specific jobs.

Presentation Suggestions:

Read the text found on the page 132.

When we think about learning most people think about a traditional classroom as the way to learn something new. Or at least a face-to-face meeting. Today we have a variety of ways to build the capacity required for the projects or jobs we want to tackle. With this activity students will gain an appreciation of that fact. This will open up a new way of thinking about "learning."

Have your students work in teams of three or four to complete the Education Plan on page 133.

Students may have limited knowledge of the ways that they could learn possible skills. Before they start the activity, have them brainstorm a list of ways that they learn things.

Ideas should include:

Face-to-face traditional classes
Online classes
Videos
Books
On-the-job training
Tutoring
Mentors
Internships
Apprenticeships

Activity:

Either individually or in groups, students look back at the list of technical skills they generated for a computer programmer and a nurse, and they develop a preliminary skill-based education plan for one of them. Each group will share their ideas with the class.

Common Core State Standards for English

CCSS.ELA-LITERACY.SL 8.1 Engage effectively in a range of collaborative discussions (one-on-one, in groups and teacher led) with diverse partners on grade 8 topics, texts, and issues, building on others ideas and expressing their own clearly.

CCSS.ELA-LITERACY.W.8.7 Conduct short research projects to answer a question (including a self-generated question), drawing on several sources and generating additional related, focused questions that allow for multiple avenues of exploration.

Chapter Ten
Your Employability Skills

Chapter Learning Objective:

Students will develop a list of employability skills that they need to enhance together with a plan for doing so.

By this point in the course, students are ready to tackle what are some very sophisticated concepts. In this chapter they will learn about employability skills, why they are so important and how they are different from technical skills. You'll want to spend time on exploring how traditional academic classrooms promote the learning of employability skills.

Students who understand the need for becoming self-directed learners in order to acquire the skills necessary to succeed, whether it is in high school, college, workplace training or in the workforce will successful students and workers. Understanding and then developing this ethos, now as a young teen, will assure they take advantage of all that is about to come their way in high school.

Your Employability Skills

Learning Objective:

Students will learn the difference between technical skills and employability skills.

Presentation Suggestions:

Employability skills for many years were known as soft skills, but this terminology undermines the critical nature of these skills. Employees get fired for their employability skills much more often than for their technical expertise. It is also the type and quality of employability skills that candidates exhibit in interviews that get them hired or that screen them out of the hiring process. Employers only interview candidates who meet the minimum technical abilities/ necessary skill sets for a position. The interview, therefore, is about candidates explaining the added value that they bring to a company through these additional employability skills.

The ability to communicate these employability skills clearly and to give concrete examples of "a time when I used this skill" is therefore of paramount importance. Students need to become familiar with the types of employability skills that employers seek when hiring. They need to be able to clearly express their individual strengths and to be prepared to share stories of situations when they demonstrated those skills. They also need to think about skill areas that they want to work on more. Students need to understand that they are developing and honing these skills throughout their lives, but that they have been working on them since they could walk and talk!

Class Discussion:

If you were an employer in a fast food restaurant, what kind of employability skills would you look for in a candidate?

Activity:

Students will circle the skills/qualities that the employer is looking for in the job announcement at the bottom of the page. You want to go over the announcement with them to make sure that they caught them all. In the next activity, they will decide whether the skills they circled are technical or employability skills.

Job Announcement

We have immediate openings for entry level Manager Trainees. We are seeking candidates with some part-time or full-time customer service experience (such as retail sales and/or banking, finance, tellers), who are hardworking and interested in learning to become a financial services manager with a growing, reputable company. We offer starting salary while training with raises when promoted. We are a fast-paced business that requires someone who is flexible, takes initiative, and is a team player. We seek self-motivated individuals looking for career advancement who enjoy a fast-paced work environment, who have excellent people skills, are self-directed learners, and are looking for an opportunity to get ahead. Experience with financial software or accounting is required. Database management and a second language is a plus. A successful candidate will be willing to train for 12 months and then relocate to one of over 200 offices.

The Difference Between Employability Skills and Technical Skills

Learning Objective:

Students will learn to identify the difference between technical skills and employability skills.

Presentation Suggestions:

You'll probably want to do the correct identification of the first couple of skills together with the whole class so that they get the idea. Then put them in small groups to complete the activity.

Activity:

Have them write "T" or "E" next to each skill they circled in the job announcement, making their choices individually before they discuss as a group.

Then have them discuss each one in their group and make sure they all agree. Come back together and go through the list with the whole class and get universal agreement.

Discuss—

Was it easy to tell the difference between technical and employability skills?

Employability Skills and Traits Checklist

Learning Objective:

Students will identify the employability skills and traits that they currently possess

Presentation Suggestions:

Students may be unfamiliar with some of these terms, so before this activity, try this:

For each of the vocabulary words, print out the following: the words themselves (on separate sheets of paper) and the definitions (on separate sheets of paper). You might want to laminate them, both to use multiple times, or with different classes.

Pin the words up around the classroom walls. Put the definitions spread out on a table in the middle of the room. Have students pick up one of the definitions, and walk around the room to identify which vocabulary words they go with. They stand next to "their" word on the wall. If more than one student chooses a vocabulary word, they have to figure out together whose is correct, and help the other person find "their" word. When everyone has finished, they read out "their" word and the definition.

Able to take constructive criticism—can openly accept feedback

Adaptable—able to change task direction

Analytical skills—solve problems by logical thinking

Communication—ability to clearly exchange information

Confident—a "can-do" attitude

Creativity—imagination

Decision making—making good choices

Dedication—committed to a task

Dependability—reliability

Enthusiasm—passion

Flexibility—willing to do different things

Focused—not able to be distracted

Hard working—conscientious

Hardy—capacity to recover quickly from difficulties

Honesty—with integrity

Initiative—ability to work independently

Innovative—capable of coming up with new ideas

Instructing—explaining something to others

Interpersonal abilities—can get along well with others

IT skills—Information Technology skills/computer savvy

Leadership—guiding others

Loyal—faithful to a company

Managing multiple priorities—ability to perform several tasks simultaneously

Multicultural sensitivity/awareness—understanding of diverse cultures

Negotiation—ability to reach an agreement acceptable to all parties

Networking—connecting with others to develop contacts

Numeracy skills—good with numbers

Organization—planning

Problem solving—finding solutions

Project management—overseeing an enterprise

Professionalism—appropriate workplace behavior

Research—systematic investigation

Self-directed learner - take initiative to learn new things

Self-motivation—working without needing supervision

Teamwork—work well with others

Tenacity—perseverance/grit

Time management—use one's time effectively

Willingness to learn—open to being trained in new skills

Activity:

Now that the students understand the vocabulary, have them work through the checklist individually to identify the employability skills and traits they current have mastered.

Assessing the Employability Skills You Have

Learning Objective:

Students will practice giving examples of times when they used their employability skills.

Presentation Suggestions:

When employers interview candidates for a job, they ask them to talk about how qualified they are for the position, and to talk about what kind of a person they are. Share the following two scenarios with the students.

"Tell me about yourself" is a common interview prompt. But many people handle this part of the interview badly. They respond by listing a lot of adjectives they think that the employer wants to hear.

For example, Eva might reply: "I'm very organized and get on well with others. I like to learn new things and I like to train others." That all sounds great, but the employer doesn't have any evidence, or reason to believe that what Eva is saying is actually true.

If instead she had said "I am very organized and get on well with others—I am in the yearbook class at school and I work with the other students to make sure that the layout looks good and we have all of the information we need. Since I joined the class I learned how to use 2 new graphics programs and I trained 3 new students on how to use them too." This gives the employer examples or evidence of what Eva has done in the past, and so the employer will be able to imagine Eva doing similar things if she were to be hired.

Activity:

Students will give examples of times when they used 5 of their employability skills that they identified in the on their checklist. In pairs, have them brainstorm and share their examples of how they've used the skills.

Planning for the Employability Skills You Need

Learning Objective:

Students will identify employability skills they would like to develop and build a plan for doing so.

Presentation Suggestions:

It may be difficult for students to come up with a plan for developing new employability skills initially, so it would be helpful to share a couple of examples with the class as a whole before they start.

For example:

Instructing—what is something they do really well that they could share with others? It could be cooking something, fixing something, creating something, etc. They could volunteer assist an instructor of cooking or art at a local children's center so they could observe their techniques.

Project management—can they put together a schedule for a project? What do they need to do and when? Can they break it down into weekly tasks and then daily tasks? Can they meet their deadlines? If something unexpected occurs, are they flexible enough to change the schedule? They can join the committee planning the prom, become part of the school newspaper editorial team, or intern with a company working on a project in your community.

Activity:

Have students select the 5 employability skills they want to develop and then work in pairs to come up with suggestions for themselves and each other for a plan to develop them.

This is an important activity to at least get the basic concept: *There is a skill you need to learn, so how you are going to take responsibility to learn it.* Expecting to get all the skills needed, whether they are technical skills or employability skills in classes that you take in school is shortsighted. Students today have to seek out at a variety of ways to get these skills.

But at the same time, their classes will provide opportunities if they just know how to identify them. Go back to the employability skills check list and talk about in what classes and activities in high school students can learn these skills. For instance getting good grades requires practicing dedication, tenacity, initiative, and probably managing multiple priorities. When working in team in class, students learn teamwork, leadership and project management skills.

Articulating Your Skills and Traits

Learning Objective:

Students will practice articulating their employability skills, with examples, in a mock interview scenario.

Presentation Suggestions:

It is sometimes difficult for us to answer the question "Why should I hire you?" Sometimes we feel shy about talking about our good characteristics, or it seems as though we are bragging.

But from an employer's point of view, if they are interviewing 6 different people for a job, and each person has similar technical skills, it is the employability skills and traits that set that person apart from the other candidates. Of course, it's important not just to list these skills, but to be able to give an example of a time when you used each one.

If you can tell a one or two sentence story about what you did with that skill, then that's what the employer will remember about you. You want to paint a picture in the interviewer's head of you doing something well.

For example:

Self-directed learner: I taught myself how to build websites so that I could help my mom sell her jewelry online.

Research: For my project as a scout I had to research a project that would benefit the community.

Activity:

Students will write a script to the question: "Why should I hire you?" It will include 3 of their employability skills with examples of times when they used them.

Then they pair up and practice using what they wrote in their scripts, but without looking at them or reading from them. They take turns being the interviewer and interviewee, with the interviewer asking "Why should I hire you?"

Self-directed Learners: a Highly-prized Skill in Today's Workplace

Learning Objective:

Students learn more about self-directed learners: why they are needed in the workplace and how to become one.

Presentation Suggestions:

For students to be successful in school and in life, in today's world of work it is vital that they become self-directed learners in order to provide job security. Why? Because technology is providing a flux in the workplace that requires workers to constantly retrain. But employers do not have the luxury to put their workers into constant training situations, and even more important sometimes the change happens so quickly a company doesn't see it coming. But usually the workers will. And those that are ahead of the game, getting the skills necessary to continue to do a good job with any change that is happening, are the workers who will not only keep their jobs, but be promoted to better positions and better pay. They will stand out for the initiative they take and that is highly prized in today's workforce.

Have students read the text on the page silently to themselves first.

Class Discussion:

What is a self-directed learner?

Why do you think self-directed learners are highly prized in today's workforce?

It will be helpful for students to reflect on a time when they already took responsibility for learning something that wasn't mandated, such as homework. They can be alert to opportunities to apply this strategy to a new skill they want to learn.

Activity:

Have the students reflect on a time when they taught themselves something. Have them write down their answers to the following prompts:

What was the skill that they taught themselves?

How did they find out about the skill? (Research)

How did they learn it? (Reading, watching a video, copying someone, taking a class etc.?)

How did they know for sure that they could perform the skill correctly? (Reflect)

When did they successfully use it again after they had initially learned it? (Recall)

Closing the Skills Gap

Learning Objective:

They learn why they need a skill-based education plan.

Presentation suggestions

Ask students to read the text silently and then as a class discuss the following:

How many of you have heard the term "Skills Gap" before?

What is meant by the term Skills Gap?

Imagine 10 years from now, as technology and science advances, the workers in the United States don't have the skills necessary to keep up with all the work that is needs to be done. What options are available to the companies that need this work done in order to not only compete but to survive?

What would be the fallout from jobs being shipped overseas to countries whose workforce has the skills?

What can you do to make sure this doesn't happen?

Chapter Eleven
Learning from the Experts

Chapter Learning Objective:

Students will explore the value of learning from experts and resources that help them become self-directed learners. Because of technology students today have readily available resources that will empower them to take more control of their own learning and understanding.

In Lesson 3 you introduced students to the videos found on the Department of Labor (DOL) web site. Now that they have personal information about careers (as they relate to their passions), it's time for students to go online and learn how to explore this DOL resource.

The notion of turning to identified experts for advice is an important one in today's world. From the Internet to a Television with scores of channels needing content, the ease of delivering information has made the selectivity of the quality of that information questionable. Individuals have to be careful who they are taking advice from.

Add to that the fact that today most adolescents turn to their peers for advice, when in actuality they may be clueless on the best way to do something or the handle a situation, it is time to bring this concept of the value and the strategies of learning from experts to their attention.

In the end not only will they get better advice, but will probably save a lot of time getting right to the heart of a topic and expediting their learning and understanding. For instance, isn't it better to watch a video that depicts what a job really does, rather than fantasize about a particular career because it sounds exciting? Choosing a book on a topic of interest, written by the recognized expert on that topic is easier and more efficient, than trying to search around the Internet to find information when in the end you don't know how accomplished the author is.

Learning from the Experts

Learning Objective:

Students will reflect on the career that appeals to them most, including how it matches their passions, traits and skills.

Presentation Suggestions:

Discuss these topics in this order:

If you wanted to learn about something, how would you go about doing that?

When students say, "Turn to the internet," ask: How do you know the web site you are querying is giving you the right answers or direction?

Why is it important to learn from experts?

What if what you wanted to learn was complex and took time? Where would you turn for advice? For instance, you wanted to learn how to become an entrepreneur and run your own small business?

The Virtual Job Shadow

Learning Objective:

Students will practice finding specific career videos of interest.

Presentation Suggestions:

As much as we'd like to be able to put students into situations in the workplace—so they can see firsthand what different careers are like—arranging for internships and job shadowing may be outside the allotment of time and resources of your school. These videos are the next best thing. In a short period of time, your students can observe what different individuals do in a variety of career settings.

Using an LCD hooked to a computer online, Demonstrate how to navigate the Department Of Labor Career One Stop web site at http://www.careeronestop.org/Videos/default.aspx

Here, they'll find over 550 short videos about different careers. Seeing is believing and these will have an impact on what the students understands a career to be. They can also be motivational for students. Once they see what a job actually does and it matches what they like and how they want to work, they will be more motivated to work hard to get the skills and training necessary to compete for a career in this arena.

Once you have demonstrated how the website works for these video, it's time for your students to try. Learning how to access, search and use this area of the Career One Stop web site is an important skill that will allow them to quickly access this treasure trove of resources, now and in the future.

Ideally you'll want to make sure that the student computers have access to audio. If students have headphones they use with mobile phones, these sometimes work by plugging them into the audio port.

If this is not possible, the videos are closed captioned for reading. But they are much more powerful with the audio included. Note that in the side bar there are also videos in Spanish.

The videos can also be assigned as homework and watched at home or at the library or career center.

We suggest that you use this DOL web site in order to introduce students to the master database of all the videos available, rather than a state or commercial platform that may limit what they can access. It's not hard to use. And it will be available throughout their life for free and that is important because of the fact that high school is not the last time students will need to or what to change careers.

Today there are some very good commercial sites with videos, but they can be costly for a school and they don't usually have the breadth of choices available. If you are lucky enough to have the resources to have a license for one of these, that's great. But also show students how to access the DOL videos so they have lifelong access.

Give them the direct web site address above and spend 5 to 10 minutes explaining the search functions for finding the videos of interest.

Activity:

Using the three careers of interest that they've identified so far, have students watch the DOL videos that correspond most closely with a specific career.

They can be found on the Career One-Stop web site at this address:

http://www.careeronestop.org/videos/careerandclustervideos/career-and-cluster-videos.aspx

Or they are easily found by going to the Careeronestop.org web site and typing in "videos" in the search box.

These videos show the types of work people do in nearly 550 careers, organized by the 16 career clusters recognized by the US. Department of Education.

> (If this web address moves—which happens when web sites are updated—
> then search, "Department of Labor career videos" and choose the videos found on the CareerOneStop.org

After watching the 3 career videos most of interest to themselves, have students reflect on what they think about each career area now that they know a little more about it, by filling in the grid.

After writing down the URL (web address) for that particular video, have them reflect on what they found most appealing or as important what they discovered that would make this not a match for them.

If you have time, ask each student to share in class what they learned about the career that they found most appealing.

Lesson Enhancement:

Ask students to share this web site with their parents or guardians. If their parents' career is included in the 550 videos, suggest they watch it together. Then, ask students to get input from their parents about what they do at work as related to the career they just viewed.

The Most Appealing Career to Me—So Far

Learning Objective:

Students will reflect on the career that appeals to them most, including how it matches their passions, traits and skills.

Presentation Suggestions:

Before students start their essay, they will need to revisit their lists of their passions, employability skills and traits. It would probably be helpful for them to write them on a separate sheet of paper to refer to as they write their essay.

Activity:

As students write about why they prefer their top career choice at the moment, they will need to explain how that choice is linked with their passions, employability skills and traits they either have or would like to develop. Have them make a list of these prior to writing their essay and then be sure to address how their preliminary chosen career addresses these.

An Important Reminder

It is important at this point, once they completed this assignment to discuss that this career is a preliminary choice based on only a few of the factors that they will have discovered about themselves and their goals. Remind them that as a freshman they'll learn so much more about themselves and the world around them. Then over the balance of their high school years, they'll continue that process so in the end the choice they make my the end of high school will be most closely aligned with what will match who they are and what they want.

From that in depth knowledge they will be able to choose an "informed" major and build a skills-based education plan that will assure they are employable in the career of their choice.

Reading the Best Book on the Topic

Learning Objective:

Using the platform of one of your student's passions, expose your students to a vital research and learning strategy that they can use throughout their lives.

Presentation Suggestions:

Just imagine if you could send your eighth graders off to high school with the ethos of a self-directed learner. Someone who can identify a topic or issue they want to study and learn and then have to tools to go about accomplishing that goal.

Self-directed learners are one of the most highly valued characteristics of employees in today's workforce. Why? Because the workplace is changing at such a rapid speed, employers need employees that stay one step ahead of change by taking charge of their own learning. They want individuals who *seek out* opportunities to keep their skills current.

There is no reason that middle grade students can't be exposed to these sophisticated strategies now.

Using the following activities, you can walk your students through the initial steps while at the same time exposing them to information that they *value* (their passion). That ensures they'll be motivated to learn.

Study Skills for Developing Self-Directed Learners

Using the Study Skills platform advocated in the ***Career Choices*** series (***Career Choices and Changes***, Chapter 12), you will teach your students the four R's of Self-directed learning:

1. Research
2. Read
3. Reflect
4. Recall

You'll want students to memorize these four activities *in this order,* so at any time in the future when they are tasked to (or want to) learn about a topic or develop a skill, they will know the steps to do so effectively and efficiently.

For the coming lesson they are going to:

Research the best book they can find on the topic they've identified as one of their passions

Read that book (which they can borrow from the library or purchase used online)

Reflect on what they've read by analyzing topics (identified in Lesson Five)

Recall by either writing a paper or making a presentation on their topic or skill

Because students are completing this project on a topic they have identified as one of their passions, you'll witness the results of the intrinsic motivation that studying a passion can elicit.

Because the topic is something that the individual truly values, by the end of the project you'll note that the quality of student writings and presentations for most students surpasses what they have done to date in your class.

Throughout the balance of not only their high school and post secondary education *but also* their time in the workforce, if students remember this four-step process and apply it whatever they are tasked to learn, they'll experience success. They will develop into life-long learners, and become the most highly prized employees today in the ever-changing world of work.

This activity could be a part of the student's final grade.

Refer to Chapter 12 of ***Career Choices and Changes*** if you'd like more information and ideas on this four-step "study skills" process. In that text, you'll also be exposed to a quantifiable Learning Plan.

Complete a timeline or pacing guide for this assignment:

Provide a deadline in a timeframe that allows for this project to be completed. Remember, you'll need to allow time for the long term project to be completed. Time for the books to be researched, ordered and delivered, and for the students to read a book-length tome. If you have chosen presentations as the final project, how long will that take? Complete a time line or pacing guide for this complete project.

If you course or section only has limited time, one suggestion would be to team up with their English Language Arts instructor or Social Studies instructor and have this content or part of this assignment integrated into their lessons.

Project: Master a new topic or skill through self-directed learning

Project Assignment:

Read the complete book you've chosen about your passion through your **research**, **reflecting** on what you've learned, and then **recall** what you've learned by either writing a paper or making a presentation to the class.

Finding the Best Book on a Topic: A Life-long Skill

Learning Objective:

How to research a subject of interest, to find the best book on the topic.

Presentation Suggestions:

Finding the best book on a topic—A life-long skill

By teaching your students how to effectively use the digital resources available on websites like Amazon, you will have provided them with a life-long skill that will propel them to becoming self-directed learners. When they understand that the knowledge of the world is at their fingertips on a keyboard, they'll have the confidence to *continue to be curious* about topics that intrigue them, or topics they must learn about to remain competitive in the workforce.

Learning the following steps will pay dividends throughout their life. Once they have learned how to do this and have experience, they are empowered to learn (or at least start the learning process) on any topic they want.

Step One: Research the best tool to learn about the topic of your choice

Ask students to review their list of passions or one of the careers they are most interested in and choose one of them about which they want to get more information or become more skilled.

Once they have identified this topic, go to the computer lab and teach students how to use Amazon.com to find the best book on that topic.

1. Log onto Amazon.com
2. In the search box at the top, click on the dropdown BOOKS to narrow their search to books
3. In the blank search box, describe the topic you want to study, for example: best book on dog care, best book on surfing, best book on cooking, best book on volleyball or whatever their chosen topic or passion is.

The results are a list of books about this topic. Give your students plenty of time to search through the titles recommended. Discuss with them:

The rating system, and how that might give them an indication of what are the best books.

Brainstorm: Which is better—two reviews that give a book 5 stars, or 200 reviews with an average rating of 3.5 stars? Show them how this works and ask them to study and analyze how to translate this data.

Once students have narrowed their choices down to three books, show them how to "go inside the book" to study the contents.

First: Study the table of contents. Does it cover topics they find relevant? Looking at a table of contents is a vital step. More than the title, it tells the reader what to expect for the money and time they'll invest in reading the book.

Second: Read a couple of pages from the text. Do they like the way the author explains things? Is it understandable to them, using vocabulary they understand?

Third: Check out the author. Are they an authority on the topic? Learning from the experts should be something to encourage in your students. This is a time to talk about all the "noise" that the Internet brings to the world. Being able to discern between the good information and the less than credible is an important skill. In today's world, where anybody can publish either online or in print, they must be careful who they learn from.

Fourth: Read the reviews. Students shouldn't rely solely on the rating system, which is just a first cut. Actually reading reviews from readers will tell them a lot about the book itself. They may determine that while the book gets a high rating, the topics covered may not be what they want.

Fifth: Consider the value. Are you going to get your money's worth? In today's marketplace, if you are going to purchase a book that you might not keep, consider purchasing it in used condition. These can be purchased and delivered for under ten dollars, in many cases.

Sixth: Digital or Paper? If there is a choice on the title they've chosen, and students have access to a tablet, they may want to purchase the digital version rather than the paper version of a book. This is a topic for discussion in class. How many students have used digital versions of books? What was their experience? If your students have a school-issued digital tablet such as an iPad, then another question could be: Which do you prefer, the digital version of a book or the paper version? Surprisingly, studies are showing that when college students are asked this question they still prefer the paper versions.

This might be an interesting research project over the course of this activity. Ask this question again at the end of the project and ask each different "camp" to defend their choice. It is still a choice that may just come down to what each individual likes best.

Sixth: Make your purchase.

Depending on the financial situation of your students, these books can be purchased by:

- Parents, as sites such as Amazon usually require a credit card or a Pay Pal account.
- The instructor, if the school purchases them. The students will have to provide the instructor with the name of the book, the author, the edition, and the cost (preferably used).

Ideally you'll have a budget to allow your students to go ahead and purchase the book they chose (perhaps within a specified dollar limit). Even if you don't, completing the research project on how to use Amazon is a valuable skill in and of itself. It will help your students become not only self-directed learners, but life-long learners.

Funding Options:

- If your school/state allows it, students can purchase their books as a consumable, just like they would art supplies. Because many used books are under $10 delivered, students may be able to fund this themselves.
- Consider asking your parent/teacher organization to provide a budget for this activity.
- Consider asking a community based organization to provide a budget for this activity. See pages 13/6–13/8 of the seventh edition of the ***Instructor's and Administrator's Guide for Career Choices and My10yearPlan.com***
- Have students conduct a fundraiser to raise funds.

Keep in mind that if you (or the school) belong to Amazon Prime, the delivery cost is free for many titles.

Why Read Books When You've Got Google?

Learning Objective:

Students understand when it is appropriate to use Google (basic questions) and when it is appropriate to turn to full length books (print, eBooks, or audio books) that provide a survey of a topic in a format that promotes in depth learning.

Presentation Suggestions:

Students are used to Googling for information that they want to find quickly, and using resources such as Wikipedia to read a summary of information on a topic. But that does not give them the same depth of information as reading a book written by an expert on a topic.

In answer to this argument, remind students that the benefit of a book-length manuscript provides them information in a cogent format, ordered intentionally in scope-and-sequence by the expert author. If they research and read the best books on *any* topic, they too can eventually become masterful at that topic. In contrast, researching a topic on Google will yield only partial amounts of information authored (usually) by a variety of people who may not have the expertise of a published author. It's piecemeal at best when one scans Google's results. Reading the entirety of an expert's work is certainly one of the most in-depth and efficient ways to learn a new topic or skill.

In addition discuss how information is put up on the internet. The bottom line is that anyone can put information on the internet whether it is correct or not. For instance in the area of health, so many people believe that have the answer for health issues and they can make convincing arguments for treatments that in some cases can be harmful. On the other hand a publisher has the responsibility and the motivation to make sure whatever they publish is factual as well as in a format the learner will find appealing. It takes a lot of work on both the author/expert's part and that of the publisher to accomplish this. Their motivation is to produce the best book on the topic so in the end a lot of people will purchase the material.

As a class take a survey: How do class members use the Internet to find information on a topic they want to know something about. When a student volunteers information, query them to determine how deep they go in that process. Are any of the topics they are looking for better served by studying in depth knowledge in a book?

When you find that example walk students through the process of looking online for that information versus going to Amazon and finding the best book on the topic. In the end they'll discover that the book may be the easiest and best resource for a complex topic.

Optional Special Project:

Project: Master a new topic or skill through self-directed learning

Project Assignment:

Read the complete book you've chosen about your passion through your **research**, **reflecting** on what you've learned, and then **recall** what you've learned by either writing a paper or making a presentation to the class.

If you have time in your coursework to have students read their books for a class assignment, here are some suggestions for your consideration. Once they have **researched** and ordered their book, using the steps of the self-directed learner:

Timing: If the assignment is to read a book about something that are passionate about, and you are teaming with one of your students' academic instructor, this project could begin as early as at the end of chapter seven. If you want to do this activity within your own course, keep in mind that this process will take a few weeks to complete.

See the detailed description on this project beginning on page 154 of the workbook.

Common Core State Standards for English

CCSS.ELA-LITERACY.W.8.6 Use technology, including the Internet, to produce and publish writing and present the relationships between information and ideas efficiently as well as to interact and collaborate with others.

Chapter Twelve

Getting Ready for High School

Chapter Learning Objective:

Students will learn about the 6 factors for student success. They will identify which of the factors they wish to improve. They will plan their next steps for self-development based on the topics covered in the workbook. They will reflect on what they have learned from the curriculum.

Keep in mind that the check list on page 165 to 167 should be used as a major grade (such as a final) for their course work, so students dedicate the energy and focus on this project in order to provide productive information for themselves and for you.

Getting Ready for High School: The Six Factors for Student Success

Learning Objectives:

Students will learn what factors they need in place to be successful students. They will be able to self-advocate for help from others in their career exploration; and they will identify people in their own networks who can nurture them.

Presentation Suggestions:

In 2012, the RP Group asked nearly 900 students from 13 California community colleges what they thought supported their educational success. The students identified the 6 areas which they regarded as critical to their success as students. Although this study was drawn from community college students, all students, including middle school students, have the same needs.

Activities:

Students will be reflecting back on some of the previous activities they have done that correspond to some of the 6 factors. In addition they will be responding to several prompts. Several of these are appropriate for class discussion, such as "What are some ways that you can make your classmates feel valued?"

As a class, read through the six factors, pausing to discuss each one.

After you read "nurtured," pause so students can reflect on and identify the individuals who will support them and encourage them. Remind your students that they'll want to be on the lookout for these individuals throughout school and on into the workforce. Later in high school, after they complete their first draft of My10yearPlan.com and they start using the app on their mobile device, they'll be able to identify their team members and start sharing their 10-year plan with them.

When addressing the success factor "connected," in addition to having students spend time on the high schools website, you might want to consider inviting to class someone to speak about the type of sports, club and organization choices available to them in high school. It's not too early for them to start thinking about how they want to be connected with their school.

Feeling "valued" is being recognized for what makes you unique. This is vital to self-esteem. Having a strong self-esteem will help students stay the course, even when the going gets tough (they get their first bad grade, they don't make the team, they aren't invited to a party). High self-esteem has been described as "the immune system of the spirit." Brainstorm with students how they have helped someone else feel valued.

After the students have read the definitions of each of the 6 factors of student success, and before they do the activity on which success factors they want to work on to be a more successful student, a mind mapping reflection activity may be helpful.

If you are not familiar with mind maps, there are many examples available on the internet. They look like different colored root systems growing outwards from a central point. They are a helpful thinking tool to organize many different ideas around a central focal point.

Activity:

Mind Maps—A valuable study skill

Divide the class into 6 groups, and assign each group one of the 6 student success factor words. In their group, have them do the following:

Step 1: Write the word they have been assigned in the center of the page (not too large!) leaving room to add their branches.

Step 2: Branch off from the central word and write down a strategy that would help someone move towards that success factor (i.e., for "focused") the first main branch might say "study strategies" (think of each branch as being like a chapter in a book). Label the branch.

Step 3: From the main branches draw some sub-branches and from those sub-branches they can draw even more branches. What they are beginning to do is create associations between ideas. So from "study strategies," they might have sub-branches for the following: "study buddies," "videos," "mind maps," etc.

Step 4: Have them draw another main branch but this time use a different color. Color helps to separate out different ideas and keeps their minds stimulated. Draw sub-branches. If they get bored at any stage, they can move on and create another branch.

Step 5: Keep repeating the above process (different colors, main branch, sub-branches).

Step 6: Voila! They have created a mind map. Remember, it doesn't have to be a work of art.

Remind your students that creating a mind map is a good way to start the process of creating a paper or research project or even writing a book. Many authors start a new writing assignment by first creating mind map for their project.

Planning for Success in High School

Learning Objective:

Students will develop a plan to assure they have addressed the six student success factors.

They want to ask themselves, do they feel:

Directed
Focused
Engaged
Nurtured
Connected
Valued

If they answer no to any of these, they want to now, while in middle school, work on ways to raise their level for those factors.

Presentation Suggestions:

Students will need to assess where they are in terms of each of the 6 factors. It may be helpful to have them write down each factor and scale from 1-5 with 1 being low levels of preparedness for success with a factor, and 5 being high.

Activity:

Then using the prompts in this activity, students can reflect on why they need to work on the low-scoring factors, and what they need to do to increase them and who can help them in the process. This may be difficult for them to think of ideas, so they may need to brainstorm in a small group or with the whole class.

If certain students feel their preparedness as it relates to the success factors are lower than they should be, you'll want to encourage that student to meet with their guidance counselor or advisor. Or depending on your school's policy you may want to alert the counseling team. It is much better to address these issues while still in middle school than to wait until high school.

Checkpoint: What Are My Next Steps?

Learning Objective:

Students will review the topics presented throughout the workbook and list areas they plan to work on. They will add a timeline and think of who will help them.

Presentation Suggestions:

This is one of the culminating activities in the workbook. Students have already done some of the work of identifying areas they want to improve as they went through the chapters and activities, but this activity gives them an opportunity to put all of those ideas together in one place, and to plan next steps—when will they do the work, and who will support them?

FINAL EXAM:

Consider using this activity as part of your final exam. Giving this activity that status will assure that students put in the time and energy this project requires.

Activity:

Students will review the previous chapters and determine what areas they would like to work on for future student success and career planning.

They may need more space to write their plans than is available in the workbook—you may want them to write/type this up as a final project, building a table in a word processing program. That way they can easily share the hard copy and the digital copy with you. And you in turn can share it with their other instructors and the guidance team.

Or you can collect the workbooks at the end of the course and copy or scan these plans so they can follow the students to high school. If you scan them, they can be attached to that students portfolio used by the school.

You can also use these plans for a student/parent conference before they matriculate to high school. Or be sure that the guidance team at the high school has a copy of these plans in the event that the high school meets with parent student teams before school starts.

> IMPORTANT: Be sure to give plenty of time to do this work. It will require doing a review of all they work they have done so far. One strategy that would work would be that when students start work in their workbook, to take them to this activity and show them what their Final will entail. That way as they work through the course material, they can continually update this plan.

What Have I Learned?

Learning Objective:

Students will take the same quiz on readiness to engage in career planning that they took at the beginning of the workbook. They will explain any changes they see from their initial responses. They will also revisit the question of what they see themselves doing in 10 years' time.

Presentation Suggestions:

Congratulate students on the work that they have done in learning about career planning and student success. Explain that it is now time to reflect on how they feel about those topics again, having completed the workbook. Emphasize that they are at the beginning of a journey to find out more about themselves and their possible futures, and that the goal is to find meaningful work that makes them happy.

Activity:

Have them retake the quiz that they took at the beginning of the workbook, without first looking back at their previous answers.

After they have answered the quiz, have them look back at their first quiz answers and note any differences. If they see a change in their beliefs about whether they can be a successful student and planner of their own career, have them explain the change.

Class Discussion:

What changes do they see in their answers?

Have them write their responses again to what they see themselves doing in 10 years' time, bearing in mind everything they have learned about in the workbook.

Class Discussion:

What do they see differently now, when they think about where they will be in 10 years?

Congratulations! You have helped students to be aware of what they need to do to be successful in school, and to start planning their own careers! Because of the care and enthusiasm you've put into to your course, they should be ready to launch into high school with the attitudes and aptitudes that will ensure that they take advantage of their next journey on their road to self-sufficiency.

Optional Long-term Project #1

Using students' passions to create self-directed learners.

Learning Objective:

Using the platform of one of your student's passions (identified in Chapter 7), expose your students to a vital research and learning strategy that they can use throughout their lives.

Background:

Just imagine if you could send your middle schoolers off to high school with the ethos of a self-directed learner. Someone who can identify a topic or issue they want to study and learn and then research to tools and resources necessary to go about accomplishing that goal.

Self-directed learners are one of the most highly valued characteristics of employees in today's workforce. Why? Because the workplace is changing at such a rapid speed, employers need employees that stay one step ahead of change by taking charge of their own learning. They want individuals who *seek out* opportunities to keep their skills current.

There is no reason that middle grade students can't be exposed to these sophisticated concepts and strategies now.

Using the following activities, you can walk your students through the initial steps while at the same time exposing them to information that they *value* (their passion). That fact ensures they'll be motivated to learn.

Study Skills for Developing Self-Directed Learners

In order to succeed in high school and life, students will want to adopt the following approach:

The Four R's of Self-directed Learning:

1. Research
2. Read
3. Reflect
4. Recall

You'll want students to memorize these four activities *in this order,* so at any time in the future when they are tasked to (or want to) learn about a topic or develop a skill, they will know the steps to do so effectively and efficiently.

For the coming lesson they are going to:

1. **Research** the best book they can find on the topic they've identified as one of their passions.
2. **Read** that book (which they can borrow from the library or purchase online).
3. **Reflect** on what they've read by analyzing topics (identified in Lesson Five).
4. **Recall** by either writing a paper or making a presentation on their chosen topic or skill.

Because students are completing this project on a topic they have identified as one of their passions, you'll witness the results of the intrinsic motivation that studying a passion can elicit.

Because the topic is something that the individual truly values, by the end of the project (in the majority of cases) you'll note that the quality of student writings and presentations surpasses what they have done to date in your class.

Throughout the balance of not only their high school and post secondary education *but also* their time in the workforce, if students remember this four-step process and apply it whatever theyare tasked to learn, they'll experience success. They will develop into life-long learners, and become the most highly prized employees today in the ever-changing world of work.

This activity could be a part of the student's final grade.

Complete a timeline or pacing guide:

Provide a deadline that allows for this project to be completed. Remember, you'll need to allow time for the books to be researched, ordered and delivered, and for the students to read an entire book. If you have chosen presentations as the final project, how long will that take? Complete a time line or pacing guide for this complete project.

For suggested pacing guides for infusing the lessons in an existing course or creating a new semester course (based in the content of this manual), see page 3/5.

You could start this project after Chapter Seven when students have identified their passions. While this some of the information is covered in Chapter Eleven (how to find a book on Amazon) if you are doing the complete project you could move that lesson ahead.

Sample Pacing Guide Rubric

Class Hour	Lesson	Notes
1		
2		
3		
4		
5		
6		
7		
8		
9		
10		
11		
12		

and so on . . .

Project: Master a new topic or skill through self-directed learning.

Project Overview:

Read a complete book about your passion that you've chosen through your **research**, **reflecting** on what you've learned, and then **recall** what you've learned by either writing a paperor making a presentation to the class.

Step One:

Research the best tool to learn about the topic of your choice

Ask students to review their list of passions and choose one of them about which they want to get more information or become more skilled.

Once they have identified this topic, go to the computer lab and teach students how to use Amazon .com to <u>find the best book on that topic</u>.

1 . Log onto Amazon.com

2 . In the search box at the top, click on the dropdown BOOKS to narrow their search to books

3 . In the blank search box, describe the topic you want to study, for example: dog car or best book on dog care, surfing or best book on surfing, best book on cooking, best book on volleyball or whatever their chosen topic or passion is .

The results are a list of books about this topic. Give your students plenty of time to search through the titles recommended. Discuss with them:

The rating system, and how that might give them an indication of what are the best books.

Brainstorm:

Which is better—two reviews that give a book 5 stars, or 200 reviews that result in an average rating of 3 .5 stars? Show them how this works and ask them to study and analyze how to interpret this data.

> One point you'll want to make to this, is that the two five star reviews could be form the authors best friends. In the event that a book has only a handful of five star reviews, your students will want to carefully study the table of contents and read some of the text to determine for themselves if this is a good book or not.

Choosing the Best Book

Once students have narrowed their choices down to three books, show them how to "go inside the book" to study the contents.

First: Study the table of contents. Does it cover topics they find relevant? Looking at a table of contents is a vital step. More than the title, it tells the reader what to expect for the money and time they'll invest in reading the book.

Second: Read a couple of pages from the text. Do they like the way the author explains things? Is it understandable to them, using vocabulary they understand?

Third: Check out the author. Are they an authority on the topic? Learning from the experts should be something to encourage in your students. This is a time to talk about all the "noise" that the Internet brings to the world. Being able to discern between the good information and the less than credible is an important skill. In today's world, where anybody can publish either online or in print, they must be careful who they learn from.

Fourth: Read the reviews. Students shouldn't rely solely on the rating system, which is just a first cut. Actually reading reviews from readers will tell them a lot about the book itself. They may determine that while the book gets a high rating, the topics covered may not be what they want.

Fifth: Consider the value. Are you going to get your money's worth? In today's marketplace, if you are going to purchase a book that you might not keep, consider purchasing it in used condition. These can be purchase and delivered many times for under ten dollars.

Sixth: Digital or Paper? If there is a choice on the title they've chosen, and students have access to a tablet, they may want to purchase the digital version rather than the paper version of a book. This is a topic for discussion in class. How many students have used digital versions of books? What was their experience? If your students have a school-issued digital tablet such as an iPad, then another question could be: Which do you prefer, the digital version of a book or the paper version? Surprisingly, studies are showing that when college students are asked this question they still prefer the paper versions.

This might be an interesting research project over the course of this activity. Ask this question again at the end of the project and ask each different "camp" to defend their choice. It is still a choice that may just come down to what each individual likes best.

Seventh: Make your purchase.

Depending on the financial situation of your students, these books can be purchased by:

- Parents or guardians, as sites such as Amazon usually require a credit card or a Pay Pal account.
- The instructor, if the school purchases them. The students will have to provide the instructor with the name of the book, the author, the edition, and the cost (preferably used).

Purchasing the Books

Ideally you'll have a budget to allow your students to go ahead and purchase the book they chose (perhaps within a specified dollar limit). Even if you don't, completing the research project on how to use Amazon is a valuable skill in and of itself. It will help your students become not only self-directed learners, but life-long learners.

Funding Options:

- If your school/state allows it, students can purchase their books as a consumable, just like they would art supplies. Because many used books are under $10 delivered, students may be able to fund this for themselves.
- Consider asking your parent/teacher organization to provide a budget for this activity.
- Consider asking a community based organization to provide a budget for this activity.
- Have students conduct a fundraiser to raise funds.
- Keep in mind that if you (or the school) belong to Amazon Prime, the delivery cost is free for many titles.

Finding the best book on a topic is a life-long skill.

By teaching your students how to effectively use the digital resources available on web sites like Amazon, you will have provided them with a life-long skill that will propel them to becoming self- directed learners. When they understand that the knowledge of the world is at their fingertips on a keyboard, they'll have the confidence to *continue to be curious* about topics that intrigue them, or topics they must learn about to remain competitive in the workforce.

Why read books when you have Google?

In answer to this argument, remind students that the benefit of a book-length manuscript provides them information in a cogent format, ordered intentionally in scope-and-sequence by the expert author. If they research and read the best books on *any* topic, they too can eventually become masterful at that topic. In contrast, researching a topic on Google will yield only partial amounts of information authored (usually) by a variety of people who may not have the expertise of a published author. It's piecemeal at best when one scans Google's results. Reading the entirety of an expert's work is certainly one of the most in-depth and efficient ways to learn a new topic or skill.

See page 4/109 for more ideas.

Step Two: Read the book

Naturally, different students will have books of different lengths, so you'll want to be sure to give enough time for this process to be completed. During the timeframe that students are assigned to read their books, keep in mind that you may not want to assign other homework.

To keep students on track and working diligently through their book, you may want to have periodic short reports (one page) written about what they've learned so far. Some students will require this accountability to stay on task.

Step Three: Reflect on what they've read by analyzing topics

This is an opportunity to give instruction on the more basic study skills strategies that individuals use to process and then retain information. Keeping in mind that individuals process information in different ways, study the different strategies and present them so students can pick the ones that work best for them. *Google: study skills, study skill tips, learning styles.*

One of the best study skills strategies when reading a book length tome, is to stop and reflect on each chapter once it is read. For each completed chapter, students could write a short paper answering these questions:

Book title:

Chapter title:

What did I learn in this chapter?

What did I find most interesting, intriguing or useful?

Questions still unanswered:

Step Four:

Recall by either writing a paper or delivering a presentation on your topic

As the old saying goes, the best way to master a subject is to teach it.

Write a Paper:

Once the book is completed, students can either write a paper about the topic they studied or make a presentation to the class about their passion and what they learned.

Some of the subjects they'll want to cover in their paper or presentation might include:

- Describe what it is that you are passionate about that drove you to read this book. What are some of the most intriguing things you discovered about your topic?
- Tell a story or give an example of something that you think most people would find interesting.
- Was the author an expert on the topic? Explain their background and why they were qualified to write the book.
- What questions do you still have about the topic, still left unanswered after reading the book?
- Do you know where you can go to find out more about this topic?
- After reading the book, are you as passionate about the topic as before reading the book? Why or why not?

Make a Presentation:

Students can deliver a presentation to the class, teaching classmates something that they've learned from reading their book. It can be a skill or a body of knowledge.

For students making presentations, consider providing instruction on how to use digital resources (such as PowerPoint or Keynote) to enhance them.

Optional Long-term Project #2

Integrated, Real-world Math to Help Students Prepare for their Freshman Transition Course

Project Overview:

Complete *Lifestyle Math* in 8th grade as a lead-in for students taking the ***Career Choices***

Freshman Transition course in high school

The ***Career Choices*** curriculum has been used in thousands of high schools for over 26 years. Each year, when teacher surveys are submitted, it is the Budget Exercise in Chapter Four that is the one they report as having such a lasting effect on their students. In short, students finalize a comprehensive budget for the lifestyle they envision for themselves and their families at age 29.

An extended and in-depth math-based version of this activity is found in *Lifestyle Math: Your Financial Planning Portfolio.*

The task for students in the project is:

- Come up with the budget for how you want to live when you are 29 years old.
- Once you do this, factor in the salary that will support this lifestyle.
- Once you know the salary required to support the lifestyle you envision, it is time to find a career that will support that lifestyle.

Eight grade students completing the 100-page math problem, found in this consumable workbook, now enter high school understanding why a good education is important to their future happiness. This increases intrinsic motivation, and therefore, academic achievement. Why? Because with this experience and information they know that in order to have the lifestyle they envision for themselves, they have to prepare themselves through education and training. Once they have envisioned a lifestyle at the level that Lifestyle Math facilitates there can no longer be the lament that according to research is the number one regret of adults: Why didn't someone tell me what is was going to be like when I was growing up, so I could have gotten a better education.

Common Core State Standards for Math

Standards for Mathematical Practice: Model with mathematics

"Mathematically proficient students can apply the mathematics they know to solve problems arising in everyday life, society, and the workplace. In early grades, this might be as simple as writing an addition equation to describe a situation. In middle grades, a student might apply proportional reasoning to plan a school event or analyze a problem in the community. By high school, a student might use geometry to solve a design problem or use a function to describe how one quantity of interest depends on another. Mathematically proficient students who can apply what they know are comfortable making assumptions and approximations to simplify a complicated situation, realizing that these may need revision later. They are able to identify important quantities in a practical situation and map their relationships using such tools as diagrams, two- way tables, graphs, flowcharts and formulas. They can analyze those relationships mathematically to draw conclusions. They routinely interpret their mathematical results in the context of the situation and reflect on whether the results make sense, possibly improving the model if it has not served its purpose."

— Quoted from www.corestandards.org
Official web site of the Common Core State Standards

The design of the *Lifestyle Math* curriculum, both workbook and online enhancement, provides a model for students to solve mathematical problems based on the lifestyle and future they envision for themselves. They'll plan for and discover one of the most important numbers of their lives: the monthly cost of their ideal lifestyle. From that number they'll be able to determine the level education to which they need to aspire. This number will have a profound effect on the energy they expend on their education over the next decade.

As you thumb through a *Lifestyle Math* workbook, you'll find diagrams, graphs, flowcharts and formulas that will inform their decision-making now and in the future. The systems they learn, based on mathematical formulas, will help to simplify the complex choices of the emerging adult.

You'll see a variety of energizers, project-based activities, and group brainstorming problems. These activities provide opportunities to differentiate instruction for students with a variety of learning styles. And, because these problems and case studies relate to their own personal issues, the activities effectively demonstrate how numeracy, financial literacy and solid math skills can be used to craft a life of their choosing.

Lifestyle Math: An Overview

Lifestyle Math is a wonderful way to personalize math. It effectively debunks many of the myths that hinder students in achieving math excellence. By making math exciting and pertinent, it proves to students that they can do math if they try. Perhaps most important, *Lifestyle Math* demonstrates to students the *personal* relevance math has in their daily lives—today and in the future. This, in turn, motivates them to apply themselves to their math studies.

Lifestyle Math is an extension of the budget exercise found in Chapter Four of ***Career Choices***. Working on the same premise, young people begin to think about and plan for the kind of life they want to have by age 2. As students move through this more detailed budgeting process, they build more than math skills. Step-by-step, as they discover the economic realities they will face as adults, the exercises increase motivation and commitment to prepare for the future *by doing well in school today*.

With *Lifestyle Math,* basic math practice comes in the guise of party planning, buying a dream car or home, and much more. Students find that math is important to their happiness and, with their newfound motivation, they realize that they can master math!

Lifestyle Math helps students by reducing the seemingly complicated life issues they'll face to the essential mathematical concepts they know. Students have the opportunity to practice addition, subtraction, multiplication, and division. They'll practice working with whole numbers, fractions, percentages, ratios, estimation, and graphing. They'll tackle real-life issues such as simple and compound interest, affordability indexes, insurance deductibles, and more.

For details see page 3/15 to 3/21 of this manual.

Making Math Exciting & Pertinent by Making It Personal!

Lifestyle Math begins by asking young people to think about and plan for the kind of lifestyle they want to have by age 29.

Then, as students work through the development of a detailed budget, they learn important financial literacy concepts as they tackle problems that support each of the **Common Core State Standards for Mathematical Practice**:

1. **Make sense of problems and persevere in solving them.**
2. **Reason abstractly and quantitatively.**
3. **Construct viable arguments and critique the reasoning of others.**
4. **Model with mathematics.**
5. **Use appropriate tools strategically.**
6. **Attend to precision.**
7. **Look for and make use of structure.**
8. **Look for and express regularity in repeated reasoning.**

By demonstrating how math is relevant to daily life, Lifestyle Math motivates students to apply themselves and helps them prove to themselves that they can succeed in math if they try.

When students do the **MATH** *& let numbers help drive their* **DECISIONS**, *they learn to make* **MONEY** *work for them!*

Lifestyle Math also helps to alleviate some of the anxiety students have about the future by discussing financial/life planning issues and reducing them to key mathematical concepts they already know. In addition to basic budgeting topics, ***Lifestyle Math*** also gives students practice with:

- Simple and compounded interest
- **Affordability indexes**
- **Insurance deductibles**
- **Planning nutritious menus and factoring daily caloric intake**
- **Saving for emergencies and retirement**
- **Estimating annual earning potential from hourly pay rates**
- **Adjusting spending when economic conditions warrant**
- **Federal financial aid and student loans**

Have questions? Contact your Educational Consultant at (800) 967-8016.

Section 5

Getting Buy-in: The First Vital Step

Topics covered in this section include strategies for:

- Meeting with the decision makers at your school or district individually and in groups to talk about starting a new program
- Developing measurable goals from the outset for implementing the program and for what the program is to accomplish.

Getting Started

Starting a new program offers a variety of challenges. Here are the main steps needed to turn your goals into reality.

1. Identify Your Goals

The first step with any new project is to identify your goals and objectives. This tried and true format will help you articulate your plan and write it as quantitative goals and objectives, providing deadlines and metrics that are measurable. This beginning roadmap will help you explain your plan to your peers and funding sources.

For examples of measurable goals see Section 7 page 5.

2. Create Buy-In Within Your School and Community

It is critical that you get all stakeholders within your school community to buy in to your new Middle School Freshman Transition effort. After you identify your stakeholders, this section provides some step-by-step strategies that have worked for other educational innovators.

You'll want to review the federal, state, and local mandates that support your goals to gauge the feasibility of funding your efforts through those sources.

Creating Buy-In for Your Course

Vision and teamwork are critical elements in any restructuring or redesign effort. However your plan to use the ***Building a Bridge to Your Future*** curriculum, you will probably have to change some of the things you've done in the past, and change is uncomfortable for everyone.

The first step toward positive and lasting change is getting the buy-in of the individuals involved. If you plan a class where you are the only instructor, you will need to get buy-in from the administration and, perhaps, a school improvement committee (parents and community members).

If you are planning an interdisciplinary curriculum, you will also need to get active buy-in from all teachers working with you, including the other instructors that touch your students' lives at some level.

You'll need to lobby for your project. Studies on the process of change suggest that the best way to get people to accept a transition is through **one-on-one discussions**. Meet with individuals over lunch or coffee and present your idea. Use this time to listen for any discomfort or concern expressed by your colleagues. You will want to address their concerns or provide possible solutions right then. If this isn't possible, get back to the individual with more information quickly.

Once you have individual bought in to the possibilities of this course, only then are you ready to schedule a meeting.

Getting Buy in from All Stakeholders

For any new program to be successful, it must have the buy-in of all stakeholders. These stakeholders include:

Faculty
Parents
District Administrators
The community
Students

Generating support for your ***Middle School Bridge*** program from these stakeholders is an important first step.

Here are some common concerns you are likely to hear:

Most of our students are going to college. Why would they need a course like this?

Fifty percent of students drop out of college or do not graduate within six years. That statistic alone should be convincing that something has to change.

In addition, studies of college students show that students who are career-focused and career-committed are far more likely to graduate from college and transition into the workforce at the level their post-secondary education prepared them for.

Today, 20% of 26-year olds live at home or are not economically independent of their parents. A recent CNN Poll showed that 48% of college graduates return home after college... and one year later 44% are still there.

Addressing the issue at it relates to economic self-sufficiency requires that students understand the necessity for a career focus and have a vision in the form of a 10-year plan to help guide them through their decade of transition...from middle school to high school, through post-secondary training or college and into the workforce as a fully self-sufficient adult.

How do we convince parents of the necessity of this type of course for their teenagers? It's an all too common refrain: "My son/daughter doesn't need this. She/he are going to college!"

In the United States, young adults who require economic support from their parents (past their schooling years) are known as Twixters according to a Time Magazine article In January 2004

In Great Britain they are known as KIPPERS. This as an acronym for:

Kids In Parents Pockets Eroding Retirement Savings

Next time you are with a group of parents who might question the importance of this type of course, ask how many of them know families whose adult children returned home after graduating from college because they couldn't find a job that would support them. Watch the hands go up and the heads nod!

Our schools use a software program or online tool to help students choose a career. Isn't that enough?

For the top 20-30 percent of your students, perhaps. For those students who probably receive this information and exploration at home or observe it within their families, a couple of hours with a software program might be enough.

But for the balance of your students, the ones who do not see the relevance in education and cannot envision a productive future with plans to realize their dreams, a couple of hours behind a computer screen is just not enough to set them on the path to the second most important decision of their lives: how they'll spend 40 hours per week for up to 40 years. Without an understanding of why they need to prepare vigorously for a career, you'll lose them.

In addition, it is important for ALL students to have the skills and information necessary so they can modify their plans when they are forced to or want to change careers. Rather than rely on software programs that are unavailable once they graduate, students will have the confidence to plot their own productive work-life course if they learn the **process** for research and decision-making. By using the real-world applications readily available on U.S. Department of Labor-sponsored websites, they'll learn where to go, to get the help they'll need throughout their lives.

They'll be empowered with the skills to manage their own career trajectories after they leave school and will not have to rely on commercial online tools that "magically" come up with career options or directions once a survey is completed.

Encouraging Your Faculty

Once you've addressed these concerns, you'll want to start orienting the faculty on the advantages of this course, all students having a My10yearplan.com and the strategies for maximizing its potential.

An involved individual, will be a committed individual. Find ways for everyone to get involved.

- Hold brainstorming sessions with all stake holders.
- Form department committees to brainstorm how to integrate course content in their lessons.
- Bring the counseling staff into provide training and support for some of the course content.
- Schedule staff development sessions for the whole school.
- Ask parents to become mentors.
- Invite district administrators and board members to students' presentations of next steps before high school (Chapter 12 of the workbook).
- Get the education reporter for the local newspaper to cover your program efforts over the year.

Spending time on the process of getting buy-in is critical to the success of any new project.

Schedule meetings of your Faculty, Parents and other Stakeholders

Once you have a team of individuals who are champions for your course, the best way to orient your stakeholders is to schedule a meeting to present your project and explain why this is vital for students today.

For sample agendas, resources, PowerPoints, short videos and other props or handouts, call Academic Innovations at (800) 967-8016.

Creating a Shared Vision

School-Wide Meeting:

Introducing Building A Bridge to Your Future Course, the 10-year Plan and the Get Focused.. Stay Focused! ™ Initiative to the Entire Faculty

Use this meeting to generate interest in the course and school-wide effort. This is a good "recruiting tool" for course instructors and committee members.

Goal of the meeting:

To help all stakeholders understand the paradigm shift required for student success:

- Why it is necessary for all students to have a career choice before a college/post secondary choice
- Why a long-range plan (10 year) rather than a traditional four year plan is necessary for all students
- How the middle school bridge programs start to prepare students for the above two goals
- How the middle school bridge program helps student master social and emotional skills required for long-term success in college and career.

Equipment or Props

- Computer with LCD projector, speakers, and screen
- Flip chart on an easel and felt tip marker
- Sets of the Building A Bridge to Your Future workbooks (at least one per table)
- Download the following short videos:
- Why A 10-year Plan?
- Flipping the College Decision making Paradigm
- Region 9 video about the Get Focused…Stay Focused! Initiative

Handouts for Participants

- Copies an overview of your course plans along with your measurable goals and objectives for your program
- Form for collecting feedback
- Three table cards (8 ½ X 5 1/2 inches) - one for each topic on each table

    Career
    College
    Major

Room Set-up

- Participants at round tables in small groups to facilitate discussion and brainstorming activities.

Lead Teacher Prep

- Read pages 2/1 to 2/8 for background information about the high school program the students will be matriculating into
- Watch the videos above
- Create the table cards: Major, College, Career

Time Allotment for Workshop

- 45 to 90 minutes

Agenda

Group Brainstorm (5 to 8 minutes)

Ask your audience to review the three cards on their table and thinking about their own experience, to place the cards in the order in which MOST students today make these decisions. What do they choose first...second and third. Give them two minutes to do that.

Then looking at the order of the cards, what order makes the most sense? In other words, what choice should be made first then second and then third so the choices are informed.

This is an activity we've done with hundreds of educators and parents. Your group will call out the right answer immediately. Stop and ask each table to discuss for only one minute why that is so.

A career choice is necessary to make an informed decision for a major. And a major choice is required to make the best choice of which college or post secondary option will be best.

But you don't have to say much about this because you'll immediately play the video:

Flipping the College Decision making paradigm.

This can be found on getfocusedstayfocued.org/gfsf_initative.php

After the video ends, ask the group to discuss this question?

Why should we be concerned about this in middle school? Aren't our students 4 and 5 years away from making these choices? Please discuss that at your table.

After only two minutes, as the groups to calls out their reasons, list those on the board.

Show the Video (10 minutes)

Why a 10-year Plan?

This can be found on be... " getfocusedstayfocused.org/why_10yrplan.php

Introduce Building a Bridge to Your Future program and workbooks (15 to 30 minutes)

- Share copies of the workbook at each table

*Provide an overview of the curriculum**

- List and discuss the points at the top of page iv of the Introduction

The *Middle School Bridge Workbook* was designed to do three very important things:

1. To prepare students to engage in the career exploration, career decision-making and career planning process in high school.
2. To raise the self-efficacy of students in order for them to believe that they can be successful in high school and beyond.
3. Introduce them to the 10 year planning process and get them enthused about this process as they enter high school.

Key points:

The curriculum was designed as a bridge to the ***Career Choices*** curriculum being offered as part of the Freshman Transition course in 9th grade in high schools across America. However, some students entering high school may find the requirement to develop a 10-year plan for high school, college/post secondary and the workforce daunting without some kind of preparation. This bridge program provides that opportunity for them to think about the importance of having a long-range plan, and to understand that without a career and education plan, they are not in control of their future lives.

Additionally, too many middle school students believe that they will not be successful in high school. But this is a fallacy. This curriculum covers numerous topic areas designed for students to understand more about their attitudes, self-concept, self-motivation and self-management. Understanding how they think about learning and life gives them important strategies so that they see how in using them, they can be successful in their future academic life and work life.

- If you have time go over the main topics of each chapter – or list the chapter titles on a powerpoint slide

Present your Course Structure: How do you plan to implement this on your campus

- Introduce your team of instructors and ask for others to get involved.

Create a long-range Vision (10 to 30 minutes)

- Show the video: Region 9 Their Get Focused…Stay Focused program (9 minutes)
- Hand out copies of your own measurable goals and objectives for the course. Choose three or four objectives.

Questions, Comments, and Commitments

Prior to the school-wide meeting, recruit support for your course and your efforts from a few key faculty members that are considered leaders and are particularly well respected. You'll do this in one-to-one meetings, say over lunch or in the teachers' lounge. At the end of the workshop, ask these individuals to share their thoughts and to outline their or their department's commitment to your program.

This agenda could also be adapted to a presentation to a parents group or the school board.

Section 6

Developing Your Pacing Guide

Lesson Planning and Pacing

Topics covered in this section include:

- Tips for making the lesson planning process easy and efficient.
- Meeting the Common Core State Standards with the ***Building a Bridge to Your Future*** curriculum.

Your Lesson Plan Pacing Guide: The Key to Success

We all know the saying, "It is far easier to edit than it is to create." Our goal is to make success as easy to reach as possible, so Academic Innovations provides a sample 45-session lesson plan pacing guides in EXEL spreadsheet format. This draft document can save you countless hours, providing the foundation and structure of your course as you develop your day-by-day, hour-by-hour lesson plans.

Over the years, we've observed that instructors who complete this planning process *before the first day of class* are much more likely to experience success with their students and feel satisfied with their course. After all, one theme of this curriculum—vision plus energy equals success— imparts the message that *planning is critical* to a life of personal satisfaction. The same holds true for any successful course.

Your Mission: Create a detailed, session-by-session lesson plan pacing guide that is easily managed.

Let's begin with the end in mind. You need to develop a customized, day-by-day lesson plan pacing guide that:

- Fits the parameters of your course
- Follows the scope and sequence of the ***Building a Bridge to Your Future*** workbook, starting in Chapter 1 and working through Chapter 12
- Empowers every student to develop a meaningful 10-year education and career plan in their ***Career Choices*** course.

An example of the recommended format is found on the Teachers' Lounge.

Step 1: Outline Your Vision and Course Parameters

An important first step is assessing your program's needs. In order to develop the best customized lesson plan pacing guide possible, you'll need to look at your proposed program, population, time limitations, educational goals, and district or state requirements.

Step 2: Consider Your Curriculum Enhancement Options

Remember to keep the ultimate goals for your course in mind. What motivated you to adopt/or consider adopting the ***Building a Bridge to Your Future*** curriculum in the first place?

- Are you meeting a particular district or state mandate for career exploration, or dropout prevention?
- Are you looking to support the Common Core with academic materials with a motivational thematic format, so that students can practice their reading, writing, and math skills while they are also preparing to transition to high school and develop a 10-year education and career plan?
- Were you intrigued by the real-world technology applications offered by the Internet enhancement LifestyleMath.com? Do these reflect your notion of how online materials should be incorporated into coursework?

Answering these questions will help you determine if and how you are going to integrate any or all of the supplemental academic or Internet-based content in your ***Building a Bridge to Your Future*** course.

You'll want to carefully review this instructor's guide, **Section 3** for various course options.

Step 3: Choose the Lesson Plan that Most Closely Meets Your Needs and Your Time Constraints

We suggest the format you'll want to use for your task of developing your pacing guide is the same as the format used for the sample lesson plan pacing guides found on the Teachers' Lounge online.

For students to develop real insights and raise their self-efficacy for career decision-making, please keep two key points in mind as you work on customizing your own lesson plans. We recommend that you:

- Dedicate at least 45 hours to the exercises in the ***Building a Bridge to Your Future*** workbook
- Work through the student workbook text in sequence (Chapters 1–12)

For additional assistance, call our Curriculum and Technical Support team at (800) 967-8016.

Step 4: Edit Your Plan to Customize Your Course

Don't look at this as a daunting task but an energizing, creative effort. The customized lesson plans that you develop, rich in content and active learning opportunities, will change the lives of your students, by changing their attitudes about their education and their futures.

Be sure to be reviewing presentation suggestions for each activity found in Section Four of this instructor's guide. At that point you can determine how much time to spend on each activity, if you want to enhance any.

Good luck, and don't hesitate to call our Curriculum and Technical Support team if we can answer any questions for you.

Tips for Managing Your Spreadsheet Editing Process

Let's say you have a semester course (or 90 sessions). You've chosen to start working from the basic 45-hour lesson plan pacing guide. This will allow you to add 45 hours of coursework. You may decide to include the English Language Arts project found starting on page 4/119 or ***Lifestyle Math***. *For information see pages 3/11 to 3/17 and pages 4/125 to 4/128.*

See Section 3 of this guide for additional information and suggestions.

Using the Sample Pacing Guide to Design Your Coursework

Okay, you've gone online to ### and located the pacing guide for 45 class sessions. You've downloaded it on your hard drive. Now the fun part starts—developing your own course by customizing your series of lessons.

While you'll want to keep the order of lessons intact, now is when you can start adding material that may be most relevant to your students. This is where using a spreadsheet makes your job easier.

The following information assumes you know the basics of EXCEL. If you don't, here's a chance to increase your skills by getting some basic instruction either from your IT department at school or better yet a student. It's not hard to learn. For instance, author Mindy Bingham learned it spending two hours with a software-based, self-paced training program in an adult education computer lab. And because you'll find it has a variety of applications in your personal life, it's worth the time to add this skill to your own list.

Tips for Customizing Your Pacing Guide Spreadsheet

Here's one technology tip you'll find very useful.

How do you get the numbering in the left hand column—the number delimitating the number of class sessions—to continue to recalculate when you add lessons? This is important, so you know when you've reached your total number of allotted sessions. For instance if you are creating 90 sessions for a semester course.

Here's an example.

Let's say you have a semester course, (90 50 minute sessions). You've decided you want to include some more in-depth work on each of the activities and the English Languages Arts project describe on page 4/117.

You are comfortable adding in specific lessons using the *insert row* functionality. BUT how do you get those pesky session numbers to change as you do this (without doing it by hand each time. . . .) Contact Academic Innovations technical support team to walk you ghrough it.

There you have it. You are ready to begin developing the customize lesson plans that will changes the lives of your students—by changing their attitudes about their education and their futures.

Good luck and don't hesitate to call our Curriculum and Technical Support Department if we can answer any questions for you.

6/6

Section 7

Instructional Strategies

The Socratic Method: Engaging students through self-discovery and questioning

To become college and career ready, students must have ample opportunities to take part in a variety of rich, structured conversations—as part of a whole class, in small groups, and with a partner—built around important content in various domains. 1

Think back to one of the most profound discoveries you've made in your life. Did someone else teach you this information? Was it the result of something someone told you? Or did you discover this truth on your own? Often, the things we hear from well-meaning friends, acquaintances, and even teachers don't mean as much to us as the things we come to realize for ourselves.

This curriculum was developed around the Socratic method of teaching, which, in simple terms, is questioning versus lecturing. Questions are posed and students then seek to answer those questions for themselves. As you thumb through the student workbook, you'll find that a large portion of the content is devoted to questions, activities, and problems designed to challenge learners to find their own answers rather than text outlining what the author feels they need to know.

The process is propelled by questions that the learners must explore as they develop their own plans for their futures. Dialectic rather than didactic, this is an ideal vehicle for a learning experience. In class, the instructor will facilitate discussions that promote more in-depth understanding.

This process of posing, investigating, and discussing questions helps develop students' critical thinking skills by prompting them to think for themselves, create their own ideas, and solve their own problems rather than relying on someone else's plan for the future. It will require the use of analysis, evaluation, and creativity to synthesize the information they've discovered—about themselves and their future options.

The curriculum's progressive format doesn't position the instructor as an authority who tells them what to learn or what to believe. As a result, students come to view the instructor as an advisor, a mentor, or a coach, which leads to a more satisfactory learning relationship for student and teacher alike.

In keeping with the spirit of the curriculum, be careful not to dictate "realistic" occupations or budgets, or to give too many opinions on the choices students make. Trust the process. The carefully designed scope and sequence of the curriculum leads students through thought-provoking questions that allow them to discover for themselves which options might truly be best for them. This is why it's important not to skip around in the curriculum but to work through it from beginning to end.

Tips and Ideas to Involve Learners

Rather than sticking to a didactic format—"read and remember"—the ***Building a Bridge to Your Future*** curriculum is organized around a series of exercises, activities, questionnaires, and models that challenge learners to find their own answers. When you thumb through the workbook, you'll see interactive exercises throughout. Recognizing that learning takes place when the learner is involved, this instructor's guide includes additional suggestions to keep your class time challenging yet exciting, informative yet fun.

If you are just starting your ***Building a Bridge to Your Future*** course, you are about to embark on an odyssey that may very well change the way you teach. Time invested in studying these classroom strategies will surely pay dividends in student engagement and achievement, not only in your ***Building a Bridge to Your Future*** class, but in any course you teach from this point forward.

Energizers

Energizers ask students to get fully involved and make good use of their own creativity! They're called energizers because they increase the energy level for the task at hand. We all know that when this happens, real learning takes place.

Energizers can take the form of art projects or utilize computer skills as students share their ideas with one another. With some energizers, students get physically involved in learning. Energizers will be the activities that your students will talk about and remember long after your class is over.

Teamwork and Cooperative Learning

Individuals who can work effectively and efficiently as part of a team are valued in the workplace. To support students as they strive to be college and career ready, the ***Career Choices*** curriculum was designed to provide opportunities to practice and perfect the skills required for teamwork, team-building, and cooperative learning.

Formalized cooperative learning strategies increase your chances of success with your group discussions and projects. You'll find a range of resources in this instructor's guide from guidelines for behavior to setting up your classroom to subtly influence the way students act.

Project-based Learning

Project-based learning is based on the idea that students retain more information when their learning is tied to a project, but it is particularly effective when that project is truly valued by the individual. A project that is relevant to students' lives generates more enthusiasm, which drives them to work harder, increases retention, and promotes skill development.

It's important that we de-compartmentalize learning. After all, isn't life just one big project? Project-based learning gives students a context for problem-solving, investigation, decision- making, and project management, and the ***Building a Bridge to Your Future*** curriculum provides a variety of opportunities for ready-made projects that can be easily incorporated into your lessons.

Optional Enhancements:

Guest Speakers

Guest speakers are the perfect way to get relevant information "straight from the horse's mouth." Guest speakers can help you bring the highest level of reality to your ***Building a Bridge to Your Future*** course.

Because so many topics are covered throughout the course, there are plenty of opportunities for you to bring in someone from the community to elaborate on what your students are learning. Counselors, retired persons, community leaders, business people, and family members are all good choices for guest speakers.

Job Shadowing

Job shadowing is a great way to give students new insights and a healthy dose of reality as they conduct career research. How can you aspire to a specific career you've never seen in action? For most students, their only exposure to the working world is what they see in their own sphere of family and friends, on TV, and in the movies. It's no wonder that the majority of students, when left to their own devices, articulate a career goal that falls within a narrow range of job titles.

Job shadowing provides students firsthand experience with careers they might find interesting. Being at work with someone experienced in a career, even for just a day, exposes students to the reality of that work and the excitement of the working world.

While the middle school course provides opportunities to experience "virtual job shadowing" in Chapter 11, if you have the resources available consider an optional real life job shadow assignment.

Cooperative Learning and Team-Building

Working efficiently and effectively as a member of a team is a prized skill in the 21st century workplace. In addition, research indicates that group learning has positive effects on student learning and achievement, self-confidence, and relationships with peers.

A classroom that incorporates a variety of cooperative learning opportunities into the coursework helps students learn important lessons.

- They develop essential life skills, including speaking, listening, negotiating, compromising, and cooperating.
- They increase their ability to accept others' points of view, receive constructive criticism, and work within a team.
- They learn to view problems as challenges and arrive at creative solutions.
- They take responsibility for their own learning by actively participating in the process.

To become college and career ready, students must have ample opportunities to take part in a variety of rich, structured conversations—as part of a whole class, in small groups, and with a partner—built around important content in various domains. They must be able to contribute appropriately to these conversations, to make comparisons and contrasts, and to analyze and synthesize a multitude of ideas.

Classroom Management Techniques for Active Learning

An instructor's most important—and challenging—role is to create a classroom environment that ensures success for all students. Using proven classroom management techniques for the active learning classroom, you can help your students stay focused and productive.

The success of group discussions can depend largely on the class environment. Every student must feel important, cared for, and supported. It is helpful if students can see each other. Arrange desks in a circle or have students sit around a table, if possible.

Before you begin, set simple guidelines for the class, including these essential ones:

- Every student must be allowed to give his or her own opinion on a topic
- No one is allowed to interrupt or discount anyone else's opinion
- The personal nature of topics requires that everyone is allowed to "pass" if called on in discussion

You'll want to point out that these same basic ground rules apply when working as a team to accomplish anything.

Assessment and Sustainability

Sample Measurable Goals and Objectives for the "Building a Bridge to Your Future" *Curriculum*

The following measurable goals and objectives are the type that funding sources (from private foundations to school boards) require. You may want to choose the most appropriate two or three for your project and edit accordingly. Include a copy of your assessment tool(s) with your proposal.

- Upon completion of the ***Building a Bridge to Your Future*** curriculum,___% of students state that they feel more confident about engaging in career exploration, career decision-making and career planning in high school as demonstrated by pre- and post-surveys.
- Upon completion of the ***Building a Bridge to Your Future*** curriculum,____% of the students in the course will have changed their attitude towards and, therefore, increased their effort in their academic subjects, as evaluated by pre- and post-surveys of their other teachers.
- In post- surveys, _______ % of graduates' parents will report a positive impact on their child due to this classroom experience.

As compared with data from the three years prior to the course introduction, after completion of the

Building a Bridge to Your Future course, among the completers:

- The attendance rate will increase by _______%
- Suspension rates will decrease by at least _______%
- Expulsion rates will decrease by at least _______%
- Average GPAs will increase by _______%

Getting this data is vital to the sustainability of your program. When you can show your stakeholders, (parents, board members and community) increasing attendance rates and GPAs along with decreasing suspension and expulsion rates, the value of this sort of work in your middle school will become evident.

Basic Ground Rules for Active Learning Classroom

The personal nature of some discussions may lead students to reveal serious problems requiring professional help. In these situations, show concern; however, avoid giving the impression that anything's "wrong" with the individual. Meet with the student after class, suggest options for getting help, and then offer any assistance he or she may need.

Make yourself available between classes or after school, and let students know you are willing to listen and lend support. This provides students who may be reluctant to share with the entire class a more private forum in which to discuss their concerns. Likewise, if a student seems to be upset during the class discussion period, suggest that he or she see you after class.

Just as there are sensitive subjects, there are sensitive students who may feel uncomfortable sharing their innermost thoughts with the class or even with you. Their privacy should be respected. Allow students to hand in written work rather than participate in group discussions if they prefer. On particularly personal or sensitive points, they may indicate that you are not to read an assignment by turning it in folded in half or by folding down those pages in the workbook. As you establish an atmosphere of trust in the class, these students should gradually become less fearful.

The curriculum is appropriate for team teaching with the school guidance counselor. You may ask him or her to participate, in particular, with your presentation of the topics Chapters 2, 4, 6, 8 and 10.

Evaluating Your Group

Is your group operating effectively?

Take time periodically to consider this question. The following checklist may be helpful. In an effective group:

Members participate somewhat equally
Members are involved and stimulated by group discussions
The environment is warm and supportive
Ideas and emotions are effectively communicated and accepted by others
Stated tasks are completed (or not completed by group agreement)
Group accomplishments are easily discernible by all members

Effective Group Facilitation Strategies

For those instructors who have more practice with a traditional lecture style of teaching, we offer a brief review of effective group facilitation.

- Group participation is essential, but students must be motivated to participate. They will generally be motivated when they:

  Have input on discussion topics
  See the discussion topics or exercises as relevant to their own lives
  Solve a problem or make a decision as a group
  Have an opportunity to voice their opinion and hear a variety of other viewpoints
  Are given tasks with a clearly defined beginning and end

  - An informal atmosphere is key. Arrange desks or chairs in a circle rather than rows so that students can see each other.
  - An atmosphere of trust is of utmost importance and an honest, respectful process ensures the best discussions. It is important to build a cohesive group in which all opinions are validated and accepted.

- Practice active listening skills and instruct the group to do the same. You may want to devote at least one class session to discussing and practicing this communication tool. In active listening, the person who is not speaking takes an active role in the dialogue. He or she never interrupts the speaker, but paraphrases what's been said when the speaker has finished. In this way, the speaker knows that he or she has been heard.

Example:

Speaker: "I like this book very much. I can really relate to the main character."

Active listener: "I'm pleased you like the book and can identify with the main character." It is also appropriate for an active listener to ask about the speaker's feelings.

Example:

Speaker: "I don't like stories with unhappy endings." Active listener: "How do they make you feel?"

Effective group facilitation and active listening will involve:

1. Restating what's been said.
2. Asking how the speaker feels.
3. Letting the speaker complete his or her statement without interruption.
4. Addressing students by name so they know they are important, you're interested in them, and you care about them.
5. Establishing a dialogue by asking questions rather than lecturing. Before offering your opinion, ask students if they want to hear it.
6. Giving students your full attention and making eye contact with the group.

7. Using humor in appropriate situations.
8. Establishing an atmosphere of trust within the group by respecting students' privacy and being honest. If you make a mistake, admit it.
9. Being clear about class rules and insisting that they be honored. State the consequences for breaking these rules and enforce them. Threats are not effective.
10. Pointing out cause and effect. Hold students accountable for their actions. Ask them to think of consequences, both immediate and long-term. This will increase their sense of autonomy and responsibility.
11. Asking for and listening to students' opinions. This will help to increase their self-esteem. Use their suggestions when you can. Let students know you believe in them.
12. Celebrating the accomplishments of the group or individuals within the group. Mentioning positive traits or behaviors, especially those of resistant or reluctant students.
13. Letting the group get to know you. Be aware of your feelings at the beginning of each class period and, if you are angry or distracted about something, let the group know that they are not the cause of your negative feelings.
14. Redirecting the discussion or taking a short break if you sense too much tension in the room.
15. Communicating your approval. When a student does or says something that pleases you, let him or her know with a word, look, smile, or nod.
16. Reminding students of the ground rules. If one or more students tend to be judgmental or try to impose their values and ideas on the group, speak with them outside the group regarding everyone's right to speak without fear of ridicule from others. You might mention that being able to get along with others and working effectively within a group are skills that are valued in the workforce.
17. Recognizing students' growing sense of self-identity.
18. Expecting students to be enthusiastic about the course. They will probably live up to your expectations as attitudes are contagious.
19. Being patient when the inevitable setbacks occur. Group learning often proceeds in a "two steps forward, one step back" fashion.
20. Never concurring with a student's disparaging remarks about family or friends. His or her ties to these people are likely strong in spite of what they say, and your remarks will not be well received.
21. Encouraging empathy by asking students to imagine how other people feel. Your example as an empathetic facilitator will help students understand the importance of empathy.

These strategies will set the tone for effective classroom discussions and will help students acquire key college and career readiness attributes, including:

> Students appreciate that the twenty-first-century classroom and workplace are settings in which people from often widely divergent cultures and who represent diverse experiences and perspectives must learn and work together. Students actively seek to understand other perspectives and cultures through reading and listening, and they are able to communicate effectively with people of varied backgrounds.

Getting Acquainted

If most of your students are unacquainted, you may want to use several group warm-up exercises during the first week of class. We suggest dividing students into pairs and having them interview each other briefly (2.5 minutes each). Bring the class back together and have students introduce their interview subject to the others. If the group seems unsure of what to ask, you might suggest some of the following questions:

If you could have any job in the world, what would it be?

If you could be any person in history, who would it be and why? Where would you most like to live? Why?

What would you consider the ideal vacation? Who is your hero? Why?

What do you like most about school? What do you like least? What are your favorite hobbies? Books? Movies? Sports?

Name a famous person you'd like to have lunch with. What would you talk about?

Typical Problems and How to Handle Them

No matter how well you facilitate your group, some students will have problems. We've listed a few common difficulties and some suggestions for dealing with them.

If a student doesn't get an opportunity to talk:

To make sure everyone gets an opportunity to be heard, break the group into pairs and have each duo come up with a certain number of ideas, answers, or suggestions. Bring the class back together and have team members take turns sharing their responses.

If someone else has already presented a student's idea or answer:

Ask him or her to rephrase the response or to elaborate.

When self-conscious students are embarrassed to speak:

Working in small groups can help these students feel safe enough to speak up. As they gain confidence, they'll be more likely to participate in larger group discussions. Don't push it, but encourage shy students with words, smiles, or nods.

When the class isn't paying attention:

A less formal atmosphere requires students to adapt to new rules and may encourage some to act up. Calmly state your own feelings of frustration and help students recognize their behavior as a response to change. Allow students to discuss their feelings and brainstorm ideas for making the group feel more comfortable and, therefore, more focused.

When the class is bored:

Boredom can be a sign that students don't understand the material or don't find it relevant. The better you know your group, the better able you will be to tailor your presentation of the materials. Breaking into smaller groups is another way to get more students active and involved.

When no one seems able to concentrate:

Lack of concentration may be due to tension or fatigue. A short stand-up break might be helpful. Alternatively, ask students to sit quietly, close their eyes, and concentrate fully on the source of their distraction for two or three minutes. When you bring their attention back to the classroom, ask them to note what they see, hear, and feel. This will help to re-focus their attention.

When there are conflicts or bad feelings in the classroom:

Conflicts between individuals should be settled out of class. The student who simply wants to complain about something should be asked to elaborate on his or her feelings and explain what, exactly, should be done about the situation. Sometimes the resolution can be as simple as placing students in different groups. But it is important that all students understand that conflicts will not be tolerated in class. In the workplace, people get fired for that sort of behavior, whether is it overt or covert.

Group Size

Whatever the size of your class, dividing into smaller groups can be advantageous. Group size varies with the task to be completed. In general, we've discovered the following:

Pairs of students:

These are ideal for sharing personal information or for encouraging students to voice personal opinions or ideas.

Groups of three:

This is a great size for discussion, especially at first, when some students may feel uncomfortable speaking in front of larger groups. Groups of three feel relatively safe. They are also good at accomplishing tasks. However, if group members are close friends, there may be too much socializing. If you use trios regularly, assign students to different groups from time to time.

Groups of four or five:

As students become more experienced and confident communicators, they can move effectively into a slightly larger group. This size is good for meetings, making decisions, or completing tasks. It also allows students to practice group problem-solving skills. Be sure the task or goal is clearly understood.

Groups of six:

To be most effective, groups of six need an appointed or elected leader, a student who is a good communicator. It might be helpful, too, to have a secretary or recorder. An easel or oversized pad can help groups of this size to stay on track. Generally, they are most effective as the course nears its end. Note: Groups of this size can easily break down into pairs or trios, which may derail completion of the assigned task. However, these smaller subsets are good for situations in which personal feedback is required.

Groups of seven or more:

As groups reach this size, they tend to become less effective. It's too easy for individuals to sit back and let others do the work.

Mixing groups:

Depending on the task, it may be appropriate for group members to know each other well or be less well-acquainted. When you want to mix the composition of groups, you might base groups on numbers or names pulled out of a hat.

Or you might give half the class questions written on 3" x 5" cards, and the other half of the class answers to the same. Have students partner with the person holding the question/answer matching their card.

One instructor kept a fish bowl by the door of their classroom. Each day as students entered they pulled a number from the fish bowl and that was their seat assignment for the day. That way, when groups were formed, the composition was always different.

Strategies for Active Learning

There are many techniques that encourage learning by stimulating enthusiasm, motivation, and group participation. Below we've listed several strategies that work particularly well with ***Building a Bridge to Your Future*** materials.

What we've heard over and over again is that it is important to use different strategies and techniques to maintain students' interest. Try not to get stuck in the rut of using only brainstorming or small work groups.

Many of these cooperative learning experiences also provide students with opportunities to practice teambuilding. This might not be obvious to them, so you'll want to remind them periodically that learning to work effectively as part of a team will pay off in the workplace.

Brainstorming

A topic is introduced to the group using a phrase such as, "Think of as many ways as you can to…" or "What are some possible solutions for…" Class members then respond verbally and suggestions are written on the board. There is no comment or criticism from the group. When all ideas have been expressed, class discussion, ranking, or prioritizing may follow.

Buzz Groups

Groups of six or fewer students share their opinions or reactions to a speaker, an article, a question, or a statement. A time limit (short in duration) should be stated at the outset to stimulate participation and competition.

Case Studies

A situation that illustrates a point or problem is presented and analyzed. Case studies are easy to relate to and can be less threatening than dealing with the same topic on a personal level. Cases may come from newspapers, magazines, TV shows, movies, books, or students' past experiences.

Debates

Debates allow students to express their opinions or examine the other side of an argument. A debate can match two individuals or two panels of students. Allow each side to present its case and respond to the other arguments, then follow with class discussion. You might set up a debate in which participants argue the position opposite their own. This is a valuable job skill.

Dialogues

Two students discuss a particular topic in front of the class. Class discussion follows.

Exercises

These can be done individually or as a group to stimulate discussion or teach skills.

Fishbowls

Group six (or fewer) students in the center of the class and have them discuss an issue or case study while the rest of the class observes from the perimeter. A class discussion may follow.

Interviews

Asking questions of people outside the class allows students to collect and synthesize data and reach conclusions concerning their topic of investigation.

Journals

This is an important ongoing activity for use with ***Building a Bridge to Your Future***. By keeping a journal, students can review their growth process now and in years to come.

Lectures or Panels

An outside speaker or group of speakers can offer detailed information, new perspectives, personal experiences, and opinions on a topic. Time should be allowed for the class to ask questions of the speaker(s).

Models

Models promote understanding by providing visual representations of certain concepts, processes, or events.

Peer Learning Groups

This is an advanced technique utilizing the leadership skills of particular students. Peer leaders must be trained for their tasks. They then lead teams of their peers through an exercise.

Role-playing

Students are asked to act out the roles in a particular situation, saying what they think their character would say. This can be an emotional experience for some individuals, so be sure to ask each role player how he or she feels both before and after the exercise.

Skits

Groups of students prepare, practice, and present short plays dealing with a given situation.

Project-based Learning

Studies have found that students retain more when their learning is tied to a project. The more relevant the project is to students' lives, the more enthusiasm it generates and the more the student retains information and skills related to the experience.

Life is one big project! It is important that we de-compartmentalize learning, particularly for the adolescent. Students can analyze, synthesize, problem solve, and manage resources all within the context of project-based learning. These models also provide opportunities for effective teamwork. You'll find a variety of activities in the ***Building a Bridge to Your Future*** curriculum that are ideal for group projects.

7/14

Section 8

Assessment and Grading

- Authentic assessments are ideal for measuring how much students have grown based on the actual work they have completed
- Checkpoint: What are My Next Steps activity in chapter 12 makes the best final exam because you can see what students have learned throughout the course by the way they can articulate their next steps.
- When assessing the coursework, look for it to be related to earlier work completed in the course, in the format the curriculum teaches, realistic, and measurable
- Assess the impact and overall success of your course using the pre- and post-course surveys.
- Complete the Annual Survey at www.academicinnovations.com/survey.html to provide feedback that can help us improve our products and services, as well as earn recognition for your school's success.

Authentic Assessments to Promote Higher-Order Thinking

The ***Career Choices*** series curriculum is unlike any other teaching tool used today. In contrast to the didactic prose of other textbooks that deliver knowledge in a passive "tell-me" format, the ***Career Choices***/My10yearPlan.com model is a series of interactive charts, activities, questions, and surveys in a carefully developed scope and sequence. Using the Socratic method of questioning (on paper) rather than lecturing (built from didactic text), this approach fosters the development of the critical thinking skills required in today's workforce.

The Middle School workbook, as part of the Career Choices series, walks students through a step-by-step process that starts the process of building a foundation for determining – with confidence—their routes to the life, career, and education plans that match their personal goals and ideals.

You can best assess what students have learned in this course by simply reviewing their work.

These include:

- Their **10-year Planning essay**, written at the beginning of the course and again at the end. Compare your students responses to see what personal growth has transpired.
- **How Ready Are You to Thank about Your Future?** Surveyed at the beginning of the course and again at the end.
- **The Most Appealing Career to Me—So Far** essay. Analyze their thinking in the informative essay. Have they incorporated information that they've learned in the course?
- **Checkpoint: What Are My Next Steps?** This could be graded as the final, as it articulates what they've learned and how they plan to use that knowledge as they matriculate to high school.

Each of the documents and plans can be graded as an authentic assessment. Evaluating the thought and consideration students have dedicated to these activities will be the best way to gauge how successful they have been in the course.

The Final

In the last chapter of the Middle School workbook students bring together all the skills and knowledge they've acquired throughout the course. It's here that they develop their plan for high school.

This provides an excellent opportunity for what is known as "authentic assessment," or the opportunity to demonstrate in a real-world context the learning and skills that have taken place throughout the course. We recommend you consider using the activities found within chapter 12 as the final exam. That way the students will give this activity the energy and focus it requires.

At the beginning of the course, from the first day if possible, provide your students with a vision of what they'll learn in your course and what is expected. Let them know that the work in chapter 12 will be their final exam.

Be sure to point out that students who diligently complete the work throughout the course will have all the information they require to complete these final worksheets. They will pull their data and plans from a variety of activities in earlier chapters.

As the end of your course nears, you'll want to make the final exam assignment at least two weeks prior to the due date of their final date. This gives your students time to thoughtfully complete the activities found in this chapter.

A word of caution:

Resist the temptation to assess students on what they memorized about career exploration and industry specifics. Lower-order multiple choice and true/false questions do not measure the higher-order skills of critical thinking, problem-solving, and synthesizing information that students learn and use in this course.

It is more important to apply principles than to simply recall them. What is essential to your students' future success – in anything they do – is the ability to apply the skills and information they learn to their own lives. If we assess what we truly want them to learn, their high school plans will be not only an important "product" of their class work, but more important, a valuable "habit" they'll embrace throughout their lives.

The Final Grading Rubric

Whether the final includes the work from all of chapter 12, or just specific exercises, these grading suggestions will be helpful. Be sure to take the following into consideration:

Relationship to earlier work completed

Does the plan reflect the carefully thought-through decisions made throughout the course?

Grounding in reality

How much thought has gone into the development of the plan and does this plan seem realistic for this student? If a student requires remedial work to get on track for his or her plan, is that included in his or her plan?

Format

Does the student use the systems and rubrics taught throughout the course? Have they taken the time to make sure their written work is grammatically correct and easy to read, something they'd be proud to share with a future employer or mentor?

Post-Course Assessment Essay

What impact did this course have on the attitudes and plans for each student?

Here is a simple way to measure the personal growth that took place for each student during the course: In class at the end of the course, ask students to rewrite their essay/narrative from the exercise "The 10 year Planning Process" found on page 11 of the workbook.

Compare this new version with the one completed at the beginning of the course. Do you see any growth in the students? Have their horizons been broadened? Perhaps their goals are more realistic for their capabilities and commitment. Do you sense better self-knowledge? Do their plans include graduation from college or the completion of a certification program to prepare for their chosen careers?

If you have access to video equipment, consider recording each student's presentation of this essay at the beginning of the course and then their rewritten presentation at the end of the course. Match up the two video files for each student and share these at a celebration event during the last class meeting. Students will be pleased with their growth, not only in knowledge and direction but also in self-confidence.

This video project can also be shared at parent conferences and presentations to the school board.

Weekly Quizzes and Discussion Questions

Multiple Choice Questions

We do not necessarily recommend multiple choice/true-false assessments as they are counter-productive to the higher-order teaching and learning opportunities of the Career Choices series pedagogy. Students do not need to memorize facts to be successful in this work. They need to use the higher order thinking skills of analysis, synthesis and strategic planning.

Grade some of the Activities

Choose (perhaps randomly) one of the activities in each chapter to grade.

Short Essay or Discussion Questions

You can also gauge your students' comprehension regularly by assigning essays that measure their acceptance and understanding of the topics in the curriculum. You'll find sample questions and essays in Section Four of this guide. You may assign questions or topics based on these as written homework, or you may choose to award points for participation in class.

Grading

There are several different grading strategies that can be used with this course. Some exercises can be graded on the basis of how much effort went into their completion. You may also wish to offer points for class participation or attendance.

The Next Steps activity beginning on page 165 of the workbook makes a good final exam. We recommend it be a "take-home" exam and that you allow the students at least two weeks to complete it. Grades can be based on how thorough the plan is and how well goals and objectives are defined.

It's always helpful to let the class know how they will be graded and what they must do to earn an A, B, C. Hand out a grading sheet on the first day of class. This sheet should outline the total graded assignments for the class and how the points are broken down. Students can then keep their own running tally and know exactly how they are doing.

Since the main goal of this course is to get students to start actively planning a satisfying future for themselves, anyone who shows enthusiasm, participates in classroom activities, and completes the assignments should do very well.

The following page provides a sample grading form. Develop a customizable version using Excel so you can easily edit topics and values to match your own course requirements.

Sample Grading Form

Total Points Possible

Attendance: Participation in discussions is important. You can earn up to [5] points per class; we meet [45] days (which totals to [225] points). To receive points for the day's attendance, you must also *complete assignments in the workbook* *<u>prior to class,</u>* *come prepared to participate in class discussions about those assignments, and be supportive of the class goals and your fellow students.* — 225

Text assignments: Comete all assignments for a total of [ ] points.

Suggested Keystone Activities

Imagining My Future Life (p. 18)	10 points	
Your Plan (p. 31)	10 points	
Your Future Happiness (p. 47)	10 points	
My Collage (p. 52–53)	25 points	
Your Successful Future (p. 58)	10 points	
The Role of High School in your Future Vision (p. 59)	10 points	
Practicing Being Positive (p. 68)	10 points	
Turning Your Behaviors in a Positive Direction (p. 71)	10 points	
Love What You Do and You'll Never Work a Day in Your Life essay (p. 77)	30 points	
Motivational Goal Setting for the Short Term (p. 90)	10 points	
Articulating your Passions (p. 91)	10 points	
Your Ideal Day essay (p. 100–101)	30 points	
What Would You Do? (p. 113)	10 points	
Starting Your List of Possible Career Choices (p. 124–125)	30 points	
Assessing the Employability Skills you Have (p. 140)	20 points	
Planning for the Employability Skills You Need (p.141)	20 points	
Why Should I Hire You? Script (p. 143)	20 points	
The Most Appealing Career to Me—So Far essay (p. 152 – 153)	30 points	
Checkpoint: What Are My Next Steps (165–167)	50 points	

Vocabulary: [12] vocabulary quizzes at points earch for a total of [120] points. — 120

Total [ ] **possible points**

A = [ ] or more points

B = [ ] or more points

C = [ ] or more points

D = [ ] or more points

How to Use Pre- and Post-Course Surveys to Assess Class Impact

Motivation is built on success. When we are successful, the feeling that accompanies success propels us to continue to strive for more success. A key question is: "How do I know if I'm successful in my efforts with the ***Building A Bridge to My Future*** course?"

One obvious way is to look at quantitative data. This includes evaluating student retention rates. Are more students staying in school and graduating? Is the dropout rate for students who have completed the curriculum lower than for students with similar backgrounds and ability in your school? Do students who go on to college stay there and graduate? Remember only 50% of those who start college complete their course of study.

Do you see an increase in students' academic achievement? Are test scores and/or grade point averages rising? As students begin to further understand the relevance of reading, writing, speaking, and computing, are they becoming more proficient in these important academic areas?

In addition to quantitative data, it's also important to look at the behavioral and attitudinal changes of your students. Are your students setting higher or more realistic goals? Upon completion of the course, do students' plans reflect higher or more realistic personal, education, career, and life goals?

Are they kinder to each other? Do they go out of their way to understand other students? Have you seen a decrease in bullying?

What about educational engagement? Do students become more engaged with their education? Do they seek out new opportunities and ways to better prepare for the future?

Finally, consider self-esteem and self-reliance. Is self-esteem high enough for students to cope with the challenges that will certainly arise as they enter adulthood? Do they feel competent to move into the adult world as emotionally and economically self-sufficient individuals?

We've all heard the saying: *Attitude is everything.* This is probably a more profound statement than most of us realize. Why? Because the motivation to learn and an understanding by students of why education is important are key indicators in predicting how well a student will do in school. If you can change reluctant learners' attitudes about the value of education, you'll see grades rise, rates of attrition decrease, and test scores increase.

How can you measure students' attitudinal shifts? The pre- and post-surveys/essays are a good place to start. It is important that the pre-survey is administered before you start delivering any of the content in the workbook and that the post-survey and essay is given at the end of the course. You'll find the comparison of student responses provides a measure of progress, both on an individual level and the overall success of your course.

These tools measures each student's change in:

- Attitude about the value of school/education
- Education goals
- Plans for the future once they complete school
- How realistic those plans are, given the effort they are willing to exert to get an education

Directions

On the first day of class, before you've done much more than introduce yourself and welcomed them to class, you'll provide each student with a copy of their workbook and ask them to write the essay on page 11 and answer the questions on page 12.

At the end of the course, as they work through chapter 12, ask them to complete these two activities again found on pages 168 and 170.

Tips for Administering the Surveys

- Before handing out the workbooks, makes sure students have a pen or pencil in front of them.
- If you feel it's necessary to read the assignment aloud for the total class, go ahead. Just be sure to provide no other commentary or editorializing that might influence their individual responses.
- During the survey allow no discussion.
- You want students to be truthful and open, so don't tie their responses to any kind of grade or class assignment for the pre survey.
- Some questions may be difficult for your students. They've probably never thought about these issues before. If you wait for all students to "finish" you may be waiting a long time.
- Do expect each student to at least try to write something.
- For the post-surveys, you'll want to allow more time for completion. By that time your students should have a lot more to write about.

Sample narrative to introduce the pre-essay—keep your directions short:

"Please get out a pen or pencil."

Once you see all have a pen or pencil, hand out the pre-course survey.

"This is a short survey that will NOT be graded so you can say what you think.

"While you may not have thought about this before, please try to respond.

"These are your thoughts only, so please no discussion or talking."

You'll have 15 minutes to work on this. Go ahead and begin.

Annual Teacher Survey and Evaluation

We invite your feedback and input. Your observations and suggestions help us continue to update and improve our curriculum and services.

If you are a course instructor, please complete the Annual Survey each year at the end of your course. In addition to getting valuable feedback, this gives us a way to provide you with the recognition you deserve. For example, we use this survey to identify potential master teachers, educators for media interviews and stories to use in our Instructor's Guides updates and online teacher interviews.

Go to www.academicinnovations.com/surveyMS.html to complete our annual teacher survey online.

The majority of the ideas and input in this manual came from completed surveys and interviews triggered by those surveys. Because your input is invaluable to us (and your colleagues using the curriculum around the country), each instructor completing our survey receives a thank you gift.

Please take time to complete the Teacher Survey.

About the Authors

Mindy Bingham

Innovative educational approaches have always been Mindy Bingham's mission. As a part-time college professor, seminar leader, author, publisher, and community activist, she has dedicated herself to improving the lives of students. In her role as CEO, social entrepreneur, and founder of Academic Innovations, she has authored or co-authored more than 20 books that collectively have sold well over 2 million copies. These titles include textbooks, instructor's manuals, trade books, and children's books. For over 30 years, she has conducted classes and workshops for administrators, teachers, and curriculum specialists, and has been a keynote presenter at regional and national conferences. She continues to consult with a variety of school districts, organizations, and national programs across the country. She has garnered numerous national and regional awards, the latest a Certificate of Special Congressional Recognition for Innovative Approaches to Curricula, in January 2015, by the United States Congress.

Karen Miles

Karen Miles, M.S., has over 25 years of career counseling and teaching experience with a range of students: community college students, international students, students on probation, students with disabilities, CalWORKs/ EOPS recipients, adult returners, middle school students, high school students, undecided students, graduate students, and community college faculty. She has a Bachelor's degree in Human Resource Management and Personnel Development; a Master's Degree in Counseling and Guidance; and she is currently pursuing a Doctor of Education Degree in Educational Leadership. She is the Regional K–14 Career Pathways Technical Assistance Provider for the South Central Coast Regional Consortium. Karen is also the CTE Career Specialist for Moorpark College, where she has worked building career pathways between high schools and the college for the last 9 years.

Tanja Easson

Along with her duties as editor of this guide, Tanja has helped educators around the country initiate and expand their educational programs as Academic Innovations' Vice President of Curriculum and Technical Support. Her creativity and talent is evident in her work with author Mindy Bingham on the development of **My10yearPlan.com®**, **CareerChoices.com**, **LifestyleMath.com**, and **The Teachers' Lounge**.

Acknowledgments

I would like to dedicate this book to my father, Michael Miles, who always supported my dreams and career, and who believed that I could do anything I attempted. I would like to thank Holly Du Bois, my 8th grade daughter, for letting me use her as a guinea pig for several of the activities. I can't wait to see what she chooses to do with her life! —Karen Miles

I dedicate this work to my husband, Jim Comiskey, who for the last 26 years has been my rock, my support, my sounding board, my muse—and my biggest critic, which drove me to find better solutions. I would like to thank both Wendy Bingham and Tanja Easson, who hold Academic Innovations together and are the force of the future of Academic Innovations. —Mindy Bingham

Ordering information—use text on page 16/6 of the CC Instructor's guide

List of all the *Career Choices* series (include GFSF titles and online enhancements) here.

If we have pages some inspirational quotes peppered throughout the last pages like in CC IG

Ordering Information

Resources, materials, and services available through Academic Innovations are noted throughout this manual. Call (800) 967-8016 for current prices.

School Orders

For faster and more accurate order processing, please include the following when submitting your order:

Purchase order number

Full book title

Quantity requested

School and/or district

Person requesting the materials

Date the materials are needed

Billing AND shipping addresses

Send purchase orders or completed order forms to:

Academic Innovations
59 South 100 East
St. George, UT 84770
Phone (800) 967-8016
FAX (800) 967-4027

Shipping

Shipping is FOB origin; shipping and handling costs will be added. Regular shipping rates are based on ground shipment. Use of other delivery methods (2nd Day Air, Overnight, etc.) will result in additional shipping charges.

Examination Copies

Examination copies of materials are available on a 60-day approval basis. If you find the titles you are reviewing will not meet your needs, return them in saleable condition prior to the end of the 60-day examination period. You will be invoiced after 60 days.

You may request a 60-day review set at www.academicinnovations.com/gfsf_60day.html or by calling (800) 967-8016.

43711172R00129

Made in the USA
San Bernardino, CA
24 December 2016